D0850754

The Knowable Future
a psychology of forecasting and prophecy

The Knowable Future
a psychology of
forecasting and prophecy

DAVID LOYE

A Wiley-Interscience Publication
JOHN WILEY & SONS
New York · Chichester · Brisbane · Toronto

Library of Congress Cataloging in Publication Data:

Loye, David.
   The knowable future.

   "A Wiley-Interscience publication."
   Bibliography: p.
   Includes index.
   1. Forecasting. 2. Social sciences—
Methodology. I. Title.
CB158.L69   300'.1'8   77-26713
ISBN 0-471-03566-1

Printed in the United States of America

10 9 8 7 6 5 4 3 2 1

To Riane
who is all my future
and to the vision and challenge
of Hari Seldon

PREFACE

It is popular to believe the future is a big mystery that may only occasionally be read by mystics and newspaper astrologers. Another belief, widespread today among scholars, is that our world is changing so fast that predicting the future is impossible. Yet every day men and women on the ''firing line'' of society—in business, governmental, and all other forms of management—are forced to predict futures to guide their planning and investments. A neglected fact with large implications is that they do so with a surprisingly high degree of success. Were this not so, all human society would collapse, for from top to bottom we are dependent on a vast network of largely impromptu decisions to do one thing rather than another. We make all such decisions by gazing ahead into the future relevant to our concern and then guessing how this future may affect us and how our decisions may affect it.

One purpose of this book is to examine the science lying behind futures prediction as a formal venture and as an informal mass activity. My findings here should be helpful to anyone who wants to improve a personal ability to foresee trends affecting his or her own future. This is no idle hope based just on theory. Out of my own background in business and management, as well as social science, I have run this new science of futurism through the mill of everyday practicality. The results are here for the reader not only to ponder but also to apply directly to his own life, either by using the IMP Quick Futures Prediction Guide in the Appendix or by launching out on his own using the book as a whole as a guide.

This is no simple ''how-to-do-it'' manual, however. For my larger purpose is this. I am, as a social scientist, deeply concerned about the failures of the social sciences—which began as vaunted tools for our survival—to meet the worsening challenges of our time. Hence, my underlying purpose is to bring together here some of the requisite knowledge for a revitalizing of social science centered on futures prediction. As a psychologist, I am by training best equipped to do this by showing how we may bring within the fold of futurism the neglected prime instrument of prophecy, the human mind itself. For incredible as it may seem, scientific futurism currently operates with neither a psychology nor the support and understanding of most psychologists, whose specialty is the *science* of mind.

This book shows: (1) how the future can be read; (2) that this is a natural capacity within each of us, scholar and nonscholar alike; and (3) that this ability can be strengthened and made more socially useful through methods for the "pooling of vision". I have divided the book into two parts to signal to potential readers a vital difference in approach. Part 1, Toward a Psychology of Forecasting, lays the necessary groundwork of fact and thought for later application. It is designed to provide both the general reader and the specialist with a common body of basic information about forecasting and a futures-relevant psychology. It introduces the reader to leading forecasters and their methods and tells how our capacity for the "pooling of vision" was accidentally discovered during the mid-1930s at the Massachusetts Institute of Technology. As so often happens, this finding was subsequently neglected, although for a time informally probed by the world-famous Gallup Poll. It explains how later formal use of Delphi and similar techniques based on this discovery have made it possible to radically increase the effectiveness of human intelligence. By such methods futurists in the early 1960s accurately predicted the energy crisis beginning in the mid-1970s, as well as the timing and specific trends for development of computer and other technologies.

Part 2, Advanced Methods and Theory, then moves on to applications—the "how to" aspects of interest to managers, professional forecasters, pollsters, and social and financial analysts. My own research and development of Ideological Matrix Prediction (IMP) is outlined. Chapter 9, in particular, tells how during the "unpredictable" 1976 presidential election I was generally able to outpredict the established polls by using IMP, successfully predicting the election of Gerald Ford as the Republican nominee, Ford's defeat for the presidency, the election of Jimmy Carter as the Democratic nominee, his selection of Walter Mondale as vice-presidential nominee, and Carter's election as president. (Spurred on by this success I am currently applying IMP to the heady challenge of stock market prediction, with hopes of reportable results by 1979.)

In keeping with rising interest in right brain "psychic" abilities as well as left brain rationality, the facts and implications of both brain half activities are explored in Parts 1 and 2. Chapter 5, for example, examines the startling use of what used to be called intuition—now psi abilities—in business and other forms of decision-making. Chapter 10 integrates theories, heavily based on modern physics, to try to unravel the mystery of how our unconscious as well as conscious minds operate in futures forecasting and prophecy.

This book is for several kinds of readers: primarily students, futurists, and forecasters in general; leaders and managers of organizations and their advisors; and psychologists and other social scientists. To serve so diverse a readership, it is written to communicate directly and informally, and, as much as possible, to be jargon-free.

For quantitative forecasters, pollsters, systems theorists, physicists, and others who are predominantly "hard" science or methods oriented, this book was written to begin to provide the psychology these scientists and practitioners are so often forced to manufacture for themselves. I characterize this need as "the hole in the prediction machine," in Chapter 3 outlining recognition of this problem by leading futurists. In Chapters 6 through 9, I develop my own new methods for "filling the hole".

For business managers, leaders, and futurists generally, the book provides an introduction to the thoughts and concepts of four leading world futurists, all founders of the still very new discipline of highly rationalized forecasting—Bertrand de Jouvenel, Herman Kahn, Olaf Helmer, and the Club of Rome scientists. This introduction is used to identify "building blocks" for an adequate psychology of forecasting. This fledgling science is then used to explore issues of salient national interest, including the baffling 1976 presidential election, and to construct the IMP Quick Futures Prediction Guide, which provides the reader with forms to use in exercising and developing his or her own powers of prediction.

For psychologists and other social scientists, the book responds to the widespread feeling among the thinkers of our disciplines that the reason for our failures to apply social science adequately to human needs is that something of vast importance is missing from modern social science. Some say it is our lack of theoretical holism. Others say it is because we are immersed in minutiae—that we are like ostriches with our heads buried in our data while the world burns. So I present here a case for viewing the neglected task of futures forecasting as a problem, central to *all* science, that could be used to revitalize social science and provide us with the new paradigms our best critics call for.

And what is the nature of the "new paradigm" that will most likely revitalize both the science and the art of forecasting and prophecy—as well as possibly social science itself? This book is the first to seriously probe the use of right as well as left brain—and forebrain—operations in futures prediction. Our reasons are these: books on rational futurism now languish on the prim shelves reserved for a few thousand scholars and practitioners, while books on intuitive futurism fairly shake, rattle, and roll on the lurid shelves reserved for the paperbacking of the "occult" to reach the millions. On still a third shelf rest the neglected books on the mind's "manager", our forebrain. This separation of the function and status of the incredible *single* power of the human mind is a disturbing reflection of the disjointedness of our lives, thought, and times. And so this book tries to bridge the gap that was both Freud's and Jung's concern: I hope to make the intelligent use of conscious mind more palatable, and of unconscious mind more respectable, to readers who need knowledge not merely of one or the other, but of *both*.

To this end, Chapter 10 attempts a theoretical reconciliation of the alienated halves, and all-too-often blinded manager, of modern mind. I hope this speculation may encourage scholars to think and practitioners to act. For what is at stake can be quickly put into hard numbers. Even slight gains in the accuracy of forecasting futures can, in cases of business management and investment, mean savings of millions of dollars, and in cases of governmental leadership, savings of millions, even billions of lives.

For encouragement and useful suggestions I am indebted to Bertrand de Jouvenel, Olaf Helmer, Herman Kahn, Barry Taff, Riane Tennenhaus, David Goodman, Carter Henderson, Don Mankin, Steven Wheelwright, Gerald Papke, Lee Perry, George Gallup, Jr., S. Colum Gilfillan, Robert Theobald, Norman Dalkey, Robert Johansen, Klaus Riegel, and Roderic Gorney. For data processing aid with the 1976 IMP study I wish to thank Larry Landers and Gary Steele, and for aid with manuscript preparation, Elizabeth Dolmat, Cindy Sprague, and Trudy Krohn. And again let me express my enduring gratitude to Silvan Tomkins and all those fine Princeton students who worked with me on this venture when it was only a wild hunch, only a determined gleam in my eye.

David Loye

Los Angeles, California
February 1978

CONTENTS

The Knowable Future
a psychology of forecasting and prophecy

Part 1

TOWARD A PSYCHOLOGY OF FORECASTING

Chapter 1

THE PROPHETIC MIND

Can we read the future? To ask the question is to defy the expert's logic, arouse the layman's skepticism, and invite the scorn of both. How can we possibly know the unknown? And yet from the earliest times, for some reason a majority of us have now and then *believed* we could.

The book of Genesis records the stream of prophecy that finds its most striking expression in Joseph's predictions of disasters based on dream analysis, prefiguring Freud and Jung. After possibly 4000 years the appeal of astrology's interpretative linking of our time of birth to positions of the stars remains unabated. Likewise the ancient *I Ching* belief in synchronicity—or bridging the gap between spiritual and physical worlds with a revealing coin toss—is again on the increase.[1]

It is easy, of course, to dismiss all this as weird exotica or as symptomatic of an abysmal lack of sophistication. But what are we then to make of the practical futurism that today underlies almost every aspect of our lives? We choose high school and college majors according to forecasts of the future job market. The roads we drive on are built—one lane between Bartlesville and Copan, or eight lanes between Los Angeles and San Diego—according to forecasts of future population concentrations. We invest in gold, or wheat, or stocks, or real estate according to forecasts of investment futures. We run for political office or cast our vote according to the poll that gives us some notion of whether our candidacy or candidate will gain office. By far the greatest part of our national budget is spent according to either the scenarios of possible future wars or projections of the swelling of the welfare rolls. We even die according to the predictions of an insurance industry based on the futures of actuarial tables. And at the other end of life we could never have taken our first steps as emergent human beings without the ability to know whether out there, in the fearful future then immediately ahead of us, solid ground or open air presented itself to our small, fumbling, and uncertain feet.

We may see, then, that, whether or not it may seem to defy logic, and whether or not we believe in biblical prophecy, astrology, or *I Ching,* in actuality every one of us daily acts on the fact that a great portion of the future *is* knowable. But again observe how hard it is for us to believe this. And so, lacking faith in ourselves, we turn to the expert. We seek out the soothsayer, the fortune teller—or the economist, sociologist, or systems analyst specializing in forecasting. While this may be generally wise, the irony is that it also appears the "gift of prophecy" is, to varying degrees, within each of us. A striking example of this propensity appears in the famous Adams family, which produced two U.S. presidents and was for four generations intimately bound to the political, economic, scientific, and educational development of the United States.[2]

Lacking supportive theory, or because this odd sort of thing didn't seem to properly fit the Adams' image, historians have been loath to mention their strange involvement with futures forecasting. However, this buried aspect of American history is of special interest today for two reasons. One is mounting concern over whether at all levels and in all aspects of society we can produce enough leadership that is sufficiently smart, tough, and rooted in humanistic values to shape the future to our advantage, rather than be overwhelmed by what we face. This was the major social concern for four generations of the Adams family. The other reason is that, as I explore in some depth in Chapter 6, the basic motivation for the Adams family's forecasts seems to prefigure the concern for human survival that, worldwide, animates most futurists today.

THE ADAMS FAMILY'S PROPHECIES

Forty-one years before the outbreak of the U.S. Civil War in 1861, while debate was raging over whether Missouri was to be admitted to the Union as "slave-holding" or "free," ex-president, now-congressman John Quincy Adams wrote a characteristically troubled letter. "The prevalent question," his quill carefully inscribed, "is a mere preamble—a title-page to a great tragic volume."[3]

This was in 1820. Somewhere in the vicinity of 1843 he added the observation that, whatever was coming, "the conflict will be terrible."[4]

Perhaps the most startling of John Quincy Adams' predictions of the Civil War, however, came in 1832, when to his general sense of future tragedy he assigned an approximate year. Discouraged by the failure of the moral authority represented by George Washington to take root in American governmental and political life, Adams lamented. He had imagined "this federative Union was to last for ages. I now disbelieve its duration for 20 years."[5] His prediction fell short only nine years.

This strain of interest then shifts to two of John Quincy's grandsons, the lawyer-social philosopher Brooks Adams and the journalist-historian Henry Adams. Writing to Brooks around 1895, Henry wondered if they "were on the edge of a new and last great centralization or of a first great movement of disintegration." He concluded the direction for the coming century was toward disintegration "with Russia for the eccentric on one side and America on the other."[6]

Over the next 15 years, while Brooks traveled the globe and Henry taught at Harvard, the two brothers became increasingly obsessed with their discussion of how beneath the surface of events one might discern the underlying forces that caused them and shaped the future. This strange dialogue of many letters and talks culminated with Henry's essay "Rule of Phase Applied to History." Posthumously published by Brooks in 1919, "Phase" is an odd mélange of Comte, Willard Gibbs' statistical physics, chemical analogies, and exponential curves. As such, it predates by many years predictive studies of Louis Ridenour, Derek Price, Anatol Rappaport, and others relating to much the same roots.[7] Applying his rule of phase to past, present, and future history, Adams felt that a "religious" phase analogous to the freezing of energy that ice represents, lasting 90,000 years, had concluded around the year 1600. This was followed by a "mechanical" phase. Analogous to the transformation of ice to water, this phase had lasted 300 years and was concluding around 1900. Looking ahead, then, Henry concluded he was passing through an unusually volatile "electrical" phase of history. Analogous to the transformation of water to steam, this phase would last only 17½ years, concluding around 1917.

Brooks, to whom Henry had sent the manuscript of "Phase" for safekeeping in 1912, felt that, in approximating 1917 as the year for an epochal shift in the course of history, Henry had predicted the catastrophe of World War I. And indeed, as Herman Kahn notes of the period out of which Adams prophesied, 1890–1914, so strong was the sense then of *La Belle Epoque*—of a good time that would be perpetuated *ad infinitum* with no catastrophe ahead—that to predict in advance a time of historical change we now know *was* fundamental, and to approximate the year, seem more than coincidence. Brooks himself, writing in 1919, predicted another major catastrophe by 1930. Was this a prediction of the Great Depression? Or nine years early, of the outbreak of World War II?

The most disquieting prediction came on the next to the last page of "Phase." On the basis of his sense of accelerating rates of technological discovery, and the exponential release of power as "mechanical" gave way to "electrical" and finally to an "ethereal" phase, Henry seems to have predicted the most terrifying event of the 1940s, the explosion of atomic bombs. If mankind "should reduce the forces of the molecule, the atom, and the electron to that costless servitude to which it has reduced the old elements of earth and air, fire and water," Adams surmised, if we "should continue to set free the infinite forces of nature, and attain the control of cosmic forces on a cosmic scale, the consequences may be as surprising as the change of water to vapor, worm to butterfly, or radium to electrons."[8]

MODERN FUTURES FORECASTING

To condense the Adams "stream of prophecy" into these few paragraphs abstracts insights that are, of course, more fuzzy in context. Moreover, they are startling only when seen in retrospect—at the time, they apparently impressed no one but Brooks, who was their chronicler. Still the sense is inescapable of a special, needed, and on occasion surprisingly reliable human power. Likewise, it does not seem unreasonable to expect that by now this power should be explainable by the science, both hard and soft, so worshipped by the Adamses from John in the 1700s to Henry in this century.

During recent years some remarkable attempts to read the future have been made by groups whose formation was motivated by several revealing concerns. The multibillion-dollar U.S. concern with national defense led to the formation of the Rand Corporation as a "think tank." This move, in turn, created the climate for developing the scenario and Delphi techniques of futures forecasting associated with the names of Herman Kahn[9] and Olaf Helmer.[10]. A concern for world peace through the mobilizing of responsible scientists and intellectuals led to the formation, with Ford Foundation money, of the Futuribles group of Bertrand de Jouvenel in France.[11] In the United States, a similar desire to focus the expertise of a wide range of scholars on problems of the future prompted the formation of The Commission on the Year 2000, headed by Daniel Bell.[12] A fourth notable development was the formation of The Club of Rome by an arousing of world industrial leadership by Aurelio Peccei and Alexander King, and the Club's sponsorship of two dramatic and well-publicized studies of the future using the power of the computer.[13]

This sketch only scratches the surface of a vast new field involving many other notable men and organizations. Of great contemporary interest, for example, is the work of Willis Harman's group at Stanford Research Institute (SRI). An amalgam of "hard science" techniques with the "soft science" perspective of humanistic psychology, Harman's projections of alternative futures are currently among the most appealing to me personally.[14] And for years now, the futurism of Peter Drucker has provided business management with provocative benchmarks for forecasting.[15] I must limit my examination in Chapter 2, however, to the four formative works that best bring the main concerns of this book into focus. One is to establish a "feel" for the technical problems of forecasting. The other is to help fill in the following alarming gap.

Advances in futurism to date have been made by men trained in the hard sciences who have been motivated by "soft" or social scientific goals—for example, the physicist Herman Kahn and the mathematician Olaf Helmer. Among social scientists there are also the beginnings of significant movement on the problem of the future among scholars of social systems, or of man's "externalities"—economists like Robert Heilbroner and sociologists like Daniel Bell. But if one turns to the fields that together include by far the greatest number of those ostensibly committed to advancing the science of man,[16] psychology and psychiatry, one encounters a startling fact. With the exception of the thrust of the Harman group at SRI and the occasional interest of psychologists Donald Michael[17], Ivan London,[18] Hans Toch,[19] Charles Osgood,[20] Milton Rokeach,[21] Don Mankin,[22] and David Goodman,[23] and psychiatrists Ira Progoff,[24] Robert McCully,[25] and Roderic Gorney,[26] psychology and psychiatry present pretty much a blank page.

In Chapter 3 I briefly examine some reasons for this alarming—and indeed socially dangerous—tendency for psychology and psychiatry to avoid the futures-reading task. In Chapters 4 and 5, however, I examine the buried side to the matter: a great past investment in a relevant psychology, as well as instances of amazing findings that have been largely ignored, not only by psychologists, but also by futurists in other disciplines.

McCLELLAND, McGREGOR, CANTRIL, AND GALLUP

Four fascinating studies applying the power of modern psychology to futures research were by the well-known psychologists David McClelland,[27] Douglas McGregor,[28] Hadley Cantril,[29] and George Gallup.[30] I examine the McGregor and Gallup studies in more detail in Chapter 4; here let me briefly note what these psychologists did, for a reason that casts light on one of the greatest difficulties facing investigators in this area. By now the reader will likely find that natural skepticism has begun to reshape his memory in ways explored by Bartlett, the Gestaltists, and other psychologists. Our report of the Adams family's "stream of prophecy," for example, is probably in the process of being safely tucked away into the mental category of "historical novelty." That is, one begins to tell oneself that, although the Adams visions are "interesting," hence worth saving in memory, they were also far back in the past, hence not relevant to here and now. Moreover, the empirically oriented reader with a sense of responsibility to method will further find himself discounting the Adams story as lacking the rigorous trappings (pre-post testing, analysis of variance, etc.) by which social science tests and legitimizes all phenomena of interest. Thus, it is essential that here at the outset we get a sense of who McGregor and Cantril were, who McClelland and Gallup still are, and what they did and found.

Douglas McGregor of M.I.T. was an especially meaningful innovator in the development of management theory. As both observers and sufferers of bureaucracy have noted, it has a dangerous tendency to drive all but the most humdrum or power-hungry out of management. McGregor was the developer of the X and Y theories of management, which shored up the embattled humanist within business and government by positing that many people work best in democratic milieus that emphasize participation in decision-making.[31] In developing his theories he was influenced by a close working association with the genius in psychology whose field theoretical approach suggestively grapples with the future, Kurt Lewin. Hadley Cantril of Princeton was an equally meaningful humanist, along with Lewin pioneering this orientation in social psychology.[32] Along with George Gallup, Cantril was also a formative thinker in the development of modern opinion polling, still the most sizable nonclinical contribution of psychology to the servicing of social needs.

In all of these men one may then detect an unusual sensitivity to the morality of our relation to our fellow beings, and in Cantril and Gallup a concern with the predictive power of testing, in McGregor a concern with the intervention power of management style. More than coincidentally, all three strains of interest come together in the person of David McClelland, long associated with Harvard University. One of the most distinguished and honored of living psychologists, McClelland is best known for his investigation of need-for-achievement motivation (or nAch, as it is known in the jargon of the trade).

THE PSYCHOLOGY OF FUTURES PREDICTION

In 1961 McClelland published a book, *The Achieving Society,* that found a limited but reliable market among teachers and students of motivation in psychology and business management. Its immediate appeal is an explanation of how need-for-achievement relates to our ability to act on our surroundings as profit-oriented entrepreneurs and thereby to the effect of individual psychology—of our personal desires and will power—on mass economic growth or decline. This is largely conveyed in terms of the necessary minutiae of psychological measurement, experiments in the modern management situation, and field studies in Germany, Italy, Turkey, Poland, Japan, Brazil, India, and Mexico. However, in a vaulting of scientific imagination now rare for psychology McClelland also cast his study within a historical framework of arresting majesty. Returning to the vast storehouse of the past that was Max Weber's laboratory, McClelland identified indicators of need-for-achievement motivation in ancient Greece, Spain in the Middle Ages, Tudor England, and pre-Incan Peru.

One especially ingenious nAch indicator McClelland's research group used was the change in decorative artwork on Greek pottery over a span of 800 years. They found that a pattern of diagonal lines, S-shaped curves, and a restless filling of space characteristic of those high in nAch changed over this span of time into a pattern of vertical and horizontal lines, undulating curves, and unused space characteristic of those low in nAch. They further found that the curve for this—and other fascinating indicators—closely matched the pattern to the expansion and contraction of trade activities for the Greeks, reflecting economic growth. McClelland then made the conceptual leap that should place this work in the most honored spot on the shelf of books for those interested in the psychology of prophecy. For he found a generational lag of the following type between what appears in man and in society. High nAch declined over generations as striving parents established easier conditions for later generations. Thus one might discern in the measurement of this motivation in man a decline that was later reflected in his society. Or by knowing the intensity of a desire affecting a specific kind of future—*with both the intensity and direction measurable by science,* as McClelland has demonstrated—we may then begin to predict the course of this future with considerably greater certainty than chance.

"For in the end, it is men, and in particular their deepest concerns, that shape history," McClelland commented in closing *The Achieving Society.* ". . .the psychologist has now developed tools for finding out what a generation wants, better than it knows itself, and *before* it has a chance of showing by its actions what it was after. With such knowledge man may be in a better position to shape his destiny."[33]

While this work of McClelland's still startles everyone who comes to it fresh, our natural skepticism, combined with the lack of a body of futuristic psychological theory or comparable studies to relate it to, quickly dissipates its impact. It is soon relegated in the memory to that convenient category of "historical novelty" to which the Adams visions may be assigned. "After all," the practical scientist must say, "this is all *ex post facto* prediction. Show me beyond question that from this point in time you can successfully predict the future and I would concede there might—and I emphasize *might*—be something to it."

The problem is this was actually done by Douglas McGregor in the 1930s—but for a long time only Hadley Cantril seems to have cared.

In 1936, in the prestigious and rigorous *Journal of Abnormal and Social Psychology,* McGregor published a study he had conducted with 400 students at Dartmouth, Bennington, and Columbia, and teachers at the Massachusetts Institute of Technology. His initiating interest was to find out to what extent people base their predictions of future events on knowledge of the area affected versus their own wishful thinking. His findings in this regard were interesting and important—we examine them in Chapter 4. But another kind of finding McGregor had not anticipated is chiefly of interest here. With some wonderment he reported that, if one simply went by the *majority opinion for those queried,* their predictions of short-term future events proved to be 100 percent correct! He asked nine questions and the nine outcomes predicted by the majority all came to be!

In the next issue of the same journal the report of Hadley Cantril's complementing study was published. Intrigued by McGregor's serendipitous discovery, Cantril had gone to the trouble of developing a much more extensive questionnaire. This time he asked for long-term as well as short-term predictions, querying people on the probable course of some political, economic, and social events over the rest of this century. He further refined the measure, not simply to try to assess the probability of certain events occurring, but also to go further and approximate the year this would supposedly happen. Also, instead of students and teachers, he queried a wider range of 205 folk from many walks of life—social psychologists, communists, lawyers, sociologists, newspaper editors, public relations counsels, economists, bankers, ministers, historians, life insurance executives, and magazine editors.

Cantril's findings added to McGregor's in defining psychological mechanisms of futures prediction. But as to the central question of the validity of his group's predictions Cantril noted realistically that this couldn't be known until some future point in time. And so these studies were forgotten. No further reference to either appears in succeeding issues of *Journal of Abnormal and Social Psychology*—nor, to my knowledge, in any of the hundreds of thousands of books and studies now comprising the literature with which today's psychologists are supposed to be acquainted.[34]

THE POOLING OF VISION

I came across these "lost works" in January of 1976. While examining the Cantril data it occurred to me that exactly 40 years had now passed since 1936 and it could be interesting to see to what extent the predictions of a majority of his study participants had come true. He had asked 15 questions ranging from "Do you think there will be another general European war?" to "How long do you think the present form of government in Germany will last?" Many of these questions about specific events also had subquestions to try to define a predicted time for the event to occur. After carefully examining questions and subquestions, I concluded there were in all 25 predictions for which either the event had occurred since 1936 or for other reasons one might judge whether the prediction had been a hit or a miss.

Despite the difficulties of long-term versus short-term prediction, and the added handicap of having to predict exact years, I found that Cantril's people had also done better than chance. They had successfully predicted the future in 16 out of 25 instances, or 64 percent of the time, against 50 percent for chance. This included an amazingly detailed prediction—in 1936, mind you—that not only would there be another general European war, but also that it would break out within the next four years. Germany would be the aggressor. It would erupt in central Europe. It would pit Germany, Italy, and Japan against France, Great Britain, the United States, Russia, and Poland. The United States would at first be neutral but then be drawn into the conflict. It would conclude with the defeat of what came to be called the "Axis Powers," ending Hitler's "1000-year Reich."

I should caution this was the successful face to a data base also including significant misses. And for a sense of the difficulties I urge the reader to carefully examine Appendices B and C, which reprint McGregor's and Cantril's questionnaires and my analysis of Cantril's findings. For prediction at best still seems a matter of guessing right more often than wrong, rather than of attaining an impossible "storybook" perfection. All this said, however, I must report an excitement like none other I have known upon first encountering the McGregor and Cantril papers. It was much like what finding the Dead Sea Scrolls must have been for the discovering archeologist—only this time in the reverse direction, this time the excitement ranging forward, to ascertain the future, rather than backward to verify the past.

Prior to encountering the McGregor and Cantril studies I had been slowly amassing notes on the work of de Jouvenel, Kahn, Helmer, and other futurists reported in Chapters 2 and 3, as well as carrying out my own futures-relevant studies reported in Chapters 7 through 9. I was not sure exactly where all this was headed, only that for some inner reason it had to be done. When I recovered from my surprise at the McGregor and Cantril groups' predictions I decided to write this book with no further delay. Every note of hope and all possible sources of strength are needed for mankind in this uncertain, dark, and querulous age. Moreover, on the individual level we need all the help we can get in our basic task of economic survival. Surely few boosts could be more hopeful or helpful than this compelling possibility: that we may, through methods for the *pooling of vision*, which these findings suggest, possess much greater power over our future than we have hitherto dared believe.

Chapter 2

THE FUTURISTS

"If it is natural and necessary, as I shall indicate, for us to have visions of the future, we owe them to an exercise of imagination which is secret, but which we can and should seek out."

Thus Bertrand de Jouvenel, possessor of one of the most subtle and far-ranging modern minds to confront the problem, states the futurist challenge.

"Otherwise," he continues in the preface to his key work *The Art of Conjecture,* "we would only be able to set one opinion of the future over against another . . . (and) only the event could decide among these opinions. But if we want henceforth to decide that one of them appears better founded, we must know how each one is bounded, on what suppositions its thought is grounded, and by what courses it has arrived at its conclusion."[1]

THE NOBLE FUTURISM OF BERTRAND DE JOUVENEL

Though futures forecasting as a sizable activity began in the United States, at the Rand Corporation in Santa Monica, our theme of the *humanism* of futurism mandates opening with de Jouvenel's views. Futures forecasting at Rand was first motivated by the concerns of warfare—the plotting of scenarios of atomic kill and overkill to guide Western defense planning. By contrast, European thinkers like de Jouvenel, who had known the horror of Hitler and World War II first hand, were earliest motivated by the desire to build a lasting peace by using forecasting to aid moral leadership in improving the worldwide condition of mankind.

De Jouvenel, a journalist, later an economist and political scientist by training—and equipped with that wealth and ease of scholarship that characterize the best French minds—did two things with major impact on futurism. In 1960 he founded the Futuribles group. Its purpose was to assess "possible futures," hence the collapsing of these two words into "futuribles" to convey a new venture for mankind with a new word. The mode of conceptual attack for this Futuribles group is especially of interest. On the surface it was an embodiment, with Ford Foundation money, of de Jouvenel's idea of a "surmising forum." Scholars in a range of disciplines, from hard through soft sciences, were asked to prepare papers examining the problems of the future from the perspective of their own field. A purpose was to regain a *holistic* grasp of the future through this intellectual coming-together of specialists, many of whom prior to this venture had well-formed feelings neither for the future nor for other disciplines. As intended, the publishing of these papers under de Jouvenel's editorship provided an explicit rallying point for other scholars beginning to search for ways to deal with the future. But more directly relevant to our main interest was an implicit impact. A vision of the future that hitherto had existed in foggy scraps in the minds of gifted men scattered throughout the world was brought together in a way *advancing consensus*. That is, one might begin to find a majority agreeing on certain things about the future, while other notions could be seen within context to be the distortions of limited views of social realities.

De Jouvenel's second major contribution was his book *The Art of Conjecture*. The importance of this work cannot be overstressed. A social danger implicit in the development of futuristic study is the possibility it could become the monopoly of a technocratic elite. That is, because so much of its advanced use requires highly specialized knowledge, and because its most efficient exercising requires the additional vast power of the computer, over time it could become the social function of a rather frightening set of "new Mandarins." These avowed superbrains would routinely jostle data from present and past through their computers and report back to the lesser brain *hoi polloi*—which would include most of us and all of our ostensible leaders—that Plan *A* was possible, but sorry, Plan *B* wasn't. The potential for rigging the results to favor the biases of the "new Mandarins" needs no elaboration.

Emblematic of this concern is the fact that most futurist works today are composed—of *necessity*—of mind-boggling projections of the trends for vast conglomerate activities such as world regional food comsumption, the rates of technological discovery since 1800, or the burgeoning of population through the year 2000. In *The Art of Conjecture* de Jouvenel deals with all this, but within the perspective of the *psychology* of the *individual*. He is, in fact, futurism's best "natural-born" psychologist (as opposed to one formally trained for the role). Repeatedly throughout *The Art of Conjecture* futurism is brought down to earth to its basic component, ourselves—to the perceptions and cognizing of fearful or hopeful men or women trying to look and think ahead.

"I project, that is to say, I cast something forward into time. What do I cast? My imagination, which jumps to a time not yet accomplished and builds something there, a *signum;* and this construct beckons and exercises a present attraction to me. Thus actions by coming before this imagined future are determined by it and prepare it rationally."[2] Or again: "It is fundamental that Ego know himself as a cause. It has even been claimed that self-consciousness comes from the experience of causing . . . Knowing myself as a cause, I contemplate various effects: Situated where? In the future."[3] Or again: "A man's actions are situated in a field of operations . . . Clearly, a man generally bases his calculations on the Map of the Present; the luminous spot that attracts him is situated both in his *personal future* and in a *social present;* he plots his path on the basis of a given map of society."[4]

Projections, imagination, rationality, fields, paths, maps—this is the language and guiding imagery of the two schools of psychology that dealt best with the intellectual requirements for a futures-relevant psychology. One is the Gestalt psychology of Kohler, Koffka, Wertheimer, Asch, and Henle.[5] Most suggestively Gestalt psychology was preoccupied with perception—with the psychology of seeing, as futurism is with *foreseeing*. The other school is the more protean "field theory" of Kurt Lewin, which, like one's forgotten sire or grandsire, underlies the microtheoretical confusion of modern social psychology.[6]

We take up this prospect of a psychology for futurism after gaining a sense of four key perspectives on the prospects for futures prediction—in addition to de Jouvenel's, the works of Herman Kahn, Olaf Helmer, and scientists sponsored by the Club of Rome.

THE PROVOCATIVE FUTURISM OF HERMAN KAHN

In marked contrast to de Jouvenel's cerebral and noncontroversial futurism is the pragmatic—and provocative—work of Herman Kahn. Since his early years at Rand and the book *On Thermonuclear War,* which inspired the film character of Kubrick's Dr. Strangelove, Kahn has periodically shocked his fellow futurists and as wide a general audience as possible. Behind the talented provocateur, however, lies an exceptionally endowed mind with notable propensities. Among futurists he is unrivaled in an ability to synthesize the knowledge of an incredible range of fields into memorably *simple* new concepts. Also in a field prone to irrealism and the wandering of mind (e.g., most utopian works), Kahn is a fierce realist.

Among the useful concepts he develops in *The Year 2000*[7] and *Things to Come*[8] is that of the "basic, long-term multifold trend." Various theorists, mainly sociological, have identified world developmental trends for secularism, humanism, bureaucracy, industrialization, technology, urbanization, population growth, et cetera. Most such concepts have been subjects of whole books in themselves. In a reduction so bold as to be almost unheard of these days in social science—and of a type crucial for the advancement of science as well as futurism—Kahn collapsed these and many other concepts into the idea of a "multifold trend" to serve as the *background* of larger sociocultural change against which one can plot the specific future (or figure) of one's immediate concern. It is also of interest that, just as for Henry Adams' mechanical phase, Kahn sees the multifold trend presently acting upon us as dating from the eleventh and twelfth centuries. As with Adams' perception of a fundamental contemporary shift of phase, Kahn makes use of Daniel Bell's concept of a shift for us into a "post-industrial society" to identify such a change within his "multifold trend."

The "surprise free projection" is another Kahnism. This is a projection of futures that doesn't contain possibilities the client for a forecast (e.g., the State Department) might find to be wildly implausible. It is "surprise free" in not containing the surprising event that may radically disrupt prior calculations, such as the assassination of President Kennedy. The Kahn lexicon also includes the detailing of possible futures in "scenarios," whereby the requirements of narrative force one to construct sequential and causality-interlinked pictures of possible future developments. From systems and computer theorizing also comes Kahn's use of the key concept of "branching points," or that like a tree or river the future may branch out in one direction rather than another at a certain point ahead of us—suggesting the importance of gauging exactly where, when, and how.

Kahn's realism is difficult to convey. In his books it is a matter of historical, sociological, and psychological insights that are impressive in the way they boldly violate conventional wisdom. More revealing than his thought, however, is Kahn's action in this regard. The development of any modern science heavily depends on the nature and stability of its organizing and funding. Seeing in futurism an entrepreneurial opportunity that offered the means of holding together a group of researchers long enough to gain the impact of sustained study, Kahn left Rand and in 1961 founded the Hudson Institute in Croton-On-Hudson, New York. With 50 research fellows and 100 consultants, the Institute is at present the largest concentration of full-time futurists in the world. Half their effort relates to U.S. defense, half to civilian needs with a large multinational corporation involvement.

In Chapter 1, I briefly described Henry Adams' theory of phases. The potential predictive power of such a view has lured many futurists over the ages (e.g., the compilers of *I Ching*, Comte, Sorokin, de Jouvenel) with as yet no fully satisfactory conclusions. Kahn, too, has dabbled in phase theory—with an outcome that has again mocked and shocked those he delights in reaching this way.

"I think there are good prospects for what the Europeans would call *la belle epoque* or, if you will, a good era similar to that experienced between the turn of the century and World War I—a worldwide period of growth, trade, peace, and prosperity on the whole, and a time, generally speaking, of optimism about the future."[9]

Kahn's development of this optimism about the future has baffled and infuriated the "doomsday" school of futurism. Behind his position lie two kinds of referents. Generally stressed by Kahn is that of "reality"—that he has simply examined the probable consequences of a leveling-off, rather than exponential increases, for population and other factors and finds most doomdsday prophecies unlikely. Behind Kahn's reading of this surface, however, lies a fascinating correspondence with earlier visions. His optimism for the twenty-first century is based on projections thematically very similar to those made in the nineteenth century by John Stuart Mill in *Principles of Political Economy* of a "stationary," or balanced, stable state society lying somewhere ahead.[10] Such a stable state is also implicit in the futurism of Karl Marx.[11] Mill's vision was again picked up by Henry Adams in "Phase," by Lewis Mumford's projecting that our "age of expansion" is giving way to an "age of equilibrium" in *The Condition of Man*,[12] and an analogue appears in Pitrim Sorokin's projection of an Idealistic or Integrated Age for man.[13]

Conventional psychology would, of course, write off such projections as nothing more than wish fulfillment or specious utopianism. And certainly this possibility does exist. The question we unconventionally pose, however, is this: If man *is* a unique futures-predicting organism, is it not likely that this propensity often reveals itself in phenomena of *consensus* or *majority* opinion? In this instance we find a very interesting consensus on the future appearance of a stable state society. It has now repeatedly emerged over at least two centuries, predictions of a specific time period beginning to appear in our time. Kahn protectively hedges, of course. But he is obviously attracted by the notion that a stable ''Augustinian age'' will come into being within 30 to 40 years, during the beginning of the next century.[14]

THE ORGANIC FUTURISM OF OLAF HELMER

''If, with Bertrand de Jouvenel, we refuse to succumb to what he calls 'the new fatalism' of passively accepting new social institutions thrust upon us by an uncontrolled technological explosion, then surely it follows that we must search for a constructive approach which will ensure to us some measure of control over the future of our society.''[15]

In these words Olaf Helmer sounds some of the concerns characterizing his work: fear of the bad consequences of technology, and a conviction that somehow social science can be wed to technology to give us a ''social technology'' offering more control of our future.

It is evident that here is an approach to the future differing from straight prediction. We are encountering the other half of the human relation to the future—the use of *intervention* to try to shape the future to our desire. These two, prediction and intervention, form the fundamental dialectic, or process complementarity, for *all* advancement into the future. This is true whether we consider the steps of a child, who predicts the nature of the ground ahead, then follows with the intervention of his feet, or the prediction of the trajectory for a rocket to the moon, followed by the blast-off.

On the social issue front, there is often such a lag between prediction and intervention that they are viewed and handled as separate operations. Moreover, as illustrated by this book, which concentrates almost exclusively on prediction, the conceptual difficulties in both areas are such that it is almost mandatory to deal with one or the other separately. But the fact remains they are conjoined in the dialectics of reality. Both de Jouvenel and Kahn have attacked the problem of prediction-intervention lag by creating forums and organizations to publicize distressing futurist information, in order to encourage intervention by the powerful to "unstress" the future. A distinction of Helmer's work is that he is the best known of a handful of futurists who have worked together to create new cohesive, small-scale, practical methods for beginning to wed the two. These methods are of special interest to me, as a psychologist, in being notably *man* based. That is, in their many forms—ranging from "slow" contact by mail, to "fast" contact by phone, to the "eyeballing" of television teleconferencing—these methods have one generally unrecognized strength in common: They are all simply means of mobilizing and organizing the very special human capacity for futures prediction this book seeks to define—hence my characterizing Helmer's approach as "organic" in being the organizing of the input to and the output from this amazing organism, the human being. The approach is further comfortingly human in having a basic form named after the famous oracle at Delphi, to whom the ancient Greeks trekked for warming or jolting views of their own uncertain future.

Basically the "Delphi technique" is little more than a sequence for inviting experts in the area in question to answer and discuss a series of questionnaires. The first mailing crudely defines the area in question. The first returns are analyzed to identify both the consensus among the experts and the range of their disagreement, or dissensus—the minority views usually kept hidden or swept aside in most open discussions. The experts are then sent a report on first results, which gives them an opportunity to see what the group thinks and to reconsider their own positions. They return this second set of questions, and the same process may again be repeated two more times. Whatever method is used, along the way much is reduced to numbers, so that at the end of this type of process one generally has a numerically descriptive prediction of futures that shows both the central tendency for majority opinion and the range for minority disagreement.

The potential power of this approach may be most quickly made evident by the use of two of Helmer's figures, which I reproduce here, for they capture concepts central to all futures prediction. Figure 2.1 shows a trend line for something that is of interest to us (whether it be growth in missiles, population, or popcorn sales). It rises from a known lower point in the past to the higher known point in the present. At this

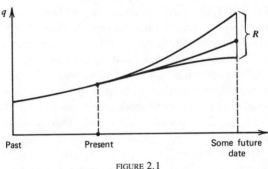

FIGURE 2.1

juncture our experts are gathered to try to predict what it will be at some date in the future. We see that a majority predict the midpoint shown within the range (R), whose upper and lower limits are defined by minority opinion. Figure 2.2 underlines this point in a way that may at first look rather peculiar but is really fetching when you consider how much statistics is collapsed herein. We see the familiar bell-shaped curve for the normal probability distribution upended and set on its side to show the precise thrust of the underlying mathematics to this crucial matter of the emphasis of majority prediction.

Helmer proceeds in his key work, *Social Technology,* to show how, in addition to the prediction of disaster, the effects of various interventions to offset the disaster may be projected, and this can provide crucial guides for social policy. An example would be the intervention of a

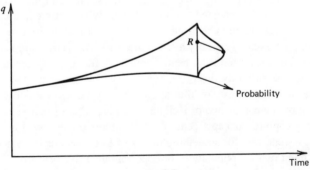

FIGURE 2.2

distribution of birth control devices and information to stave off the predicted disaster of an unchecked world population explosion. The practical thrust of these methods is, one, they provide a way of maximizing human futures predictive power, and two, their results are laden with the authority and force of both expert and group opinion, scientifically analyzed, with generally a computer involvement, as against the much less convincing weight of opinion of any one of us or the unaided group.

As Kahn left Rand to form The Hudson Institute, Helmer left to co-found The Institute for the Future, now an important futures research group located in Menlo Park near Stanford Research Institute. Later, Helmer became associated with another formative West Coast institution, The Center for Futures Research at the University of Southern California.[16] Though both men began at Rand, it would be hard to visualize two more different styles. Kahn's futurism is impressive in its massive wealth of socio-cultural-historical-psychological detail and its marshaling of vast patterns of movement. By contrast Helmer's is the spare, stripped-to-the-bone style of the mathematically oriented engineer. Both lead to different ways of structuring and synthesizing the output of expertise—Kahn's to synthesis through self, his own integrative self and the selves of others at The Hudson Institute; Helmer's to synthesis through ostensibly self-transcending methodologies.

It is also notable that where by the mid-1970s Kahn was optimistic about the future, in the early 1960s Helmer's pioneering group of Delphi-predicting experts foresaw neither optimism nor pessimism but mixed possibilities ahead. These experts included de Jouvenel, noted futurist Dennis Gabor, and the brilliant science fictionists Isaac Azimov and Arthur C. Clarke. They felt that the nuclear war threat, social upheaval through the explosive growth of automation, and the problems posed by biological advancement in extending and shaping lives through genetic control were areas in which "a major effort to seek improved ways of forestalling . . . disaster is mandatory." They also foresaw a major challenge in world inequalities of resource distribution—food, fuel, raw materials. *In other words, in the early 1960s, by using Delphi methods, this group foresaw the energy and world food crises that came to be in the 1970s.* However, their concern on this front was, in the futurist perspective, largely "short run." They were optimistic that by 2000 or 2100, despite a burgeoning population, these problems could be solved. They also foresaw a planet *not* inundated with our proliferating progeny stacked atop one another like cheeses in a warehouse, but rather a drop-off in the explosive rate of world population growth that has prevailed since 1850.

THE COMPUTERIZED FUTURISM OF THE CLUB OF ROME

We pride ourselves that America was founded following the consequences of the "shot heard round the world." By this token the Club of Rome's first work, the *Limits to Growth* study of a group headed by Dennis Meadows, was a *jolt* felt round the world. From the earlier times of William Blake, Parson Malthus, Henry Adams, and H. G. Wells, pessimists have predicted doom rather than utopia for mankind. The horror of Hiroshima, Nagasaki, and Alamogordo, however, like stones cast into a pool of waiting fear, widened doom prediction into a general pastime. In 1972 this powerful latent attitude was radically crystallized with the publication of *Limits to Growth*. For here in an intellectual book, not dropped into the obscurity of the scholarly press but receiving worldwide publicity and publication, was reported the ultimate confirmation of everyone's worst fears. By consulting the binary magic of the frightening new computer power a group of leading scientists had found out exactly when we were all to die. At approximately the year 2100 we would all perish through a gory combination of starvation, suffocation, and being crushed to death by the sardine-like stacking of bodies over the face of the earth. Moreover, no matter what they did to the computer, it gave the same answer. Eat, drink, and be merry, for there is no tomorrow.

This was, of course, more a fantasy revealing the intensity of our fears than what the book said or the scientists actually found. They did report that the computer projections were of doom—*but only if we did not take steps to stave off disaster*. In other words, they predicted doom if we did not properly intervene. Moreover, the main doom they uncovered was not the old biblical vision of Armageddon, which no doubt fueled the popular fantasy. It was the doom of hopes linked to unchecked growth—dreams of ever larger trade territories, greater profits, more and more gadgets, et cetera. In short, their real message was, as the *title* of the book clearly stated, that there are limits to the population and economic growth this planet can sustain; these limits will probably be reached by 2100; and we face a mounting series of crises if we don't change our ways.

Two future aspects of this study are notable here. One is that its nonpsychologist, computer scientist authors identify the problems of values change as of major importance for our social survival (as opposed to animal or species survival). This is a problem for applied psychology and psychiatry about which relatively little is being done.

The other aspect is this generally overlooked point about the study. Having identified limits to growth as the problem, Meadows and team then moved on to examine the prospects for John Stuart Mills' "stationary" or equilibrium society as the solution. Moreover, the authors note that the idea's forebears also included Plato, Aristotle, Malthus, and more recently Harrison Brown and Kenneth Boulding. Again, we must ask whether this may be an instance of consensus through the predicting capacity of mankind at work. We would also note that the authors outline many problems for the transition to and sustaining of an age of equilibrium for the attention of psychologists. Yet again we must report that few even recognize the challenge, much less have begun to do anything about it.

While many reacted to *Limits to Growth* with horrified acceptance, others rose automatically to attack and, if possible, reject it. A conclusion (mirroring Meadows' own reservations) was that the model used was inadequate. This prompted the funding by the Volkswagen Foundation of The Club of Rome's second major computerized study. This time Mihajlo Mesarovic and Eduard Pestel collaborated with an international team of experts to construct a computer model handling 100,000 variable relationships, as opposed to a few hundred for other comparable world models. The results were reported in a noble and eloquent book—which therefore seized no headlines—*Mankind at the Turning Point.*

"This book helps us realize that we are on a fatal course. How can a true world community emerge, or even our present human society survive when it is ridden by profound and intolerable injustices, overpopulation and megafamines, while it is crippled by energy and materials shortages, and eaten up by inflation? What explosions or breakdowns will occur, and where and when, now that nuclear war technology and civil violence are outrunning the pace of political wisdom and stability? The odds seem against man. Yet we are moderately hopeful. The winds of change have begun to blow."[17]

The voice is that of a remarkable futurist, Aurelio Peccei-

—economist, director of the management consulting firm Italconsult, consultant to Fiat and Olivetti, chief catalyst and co-founder of The Club of Rome. Earlier we noted the defense and moral motivations animating the work of de Jouvenel, Kahn, and Helmer. The Club of Rome is of great interest because it represents the arousal of world industrial leadership—the animating perception of business statesmen that, if the rest of us go, they, too, go down the drain; or more loftily, that there can be no enduring wealth unless the system producing it is stablilized and the wealth shared. The hopeful and exciting thing about this group is that it represents the arousal of the chosen few whose hands actually occasionally brush the levers of power, the arousal of *leadership* as well as scholarship. This power base adds to The Club of Rome works an interventionist dimension of meaning.

Of *Mankind at the Turning Point*'s many findings and concepts, two are particularly notable. One is the development of the concept of *organic* growth, which serves as the centering image not only for the thinking of Mesarovic and Pestel, but also, in fascinating ways, for their intricate computer model. "Two types of growth processes are of interest here: one is *undifferentiated growth*, the other is *organic growth*, or growth with differentiation."[18] The first type (to paraphrase their argument) has brought us to the verge of world disaster; the second is what we must encourage by applying thought to human affairs from a world perspective. One is cancer; the other is growth controlled by an overall specific form, as with human beings or trees.

The other useful matter is their strong feeling (held by most futurists) for scenarios, or projection of *alternative* futures, as the preferred means for "predicting" long-term social futures. The idea fits well with the concept of organic growth. The futurist's task then becomes not simply to try to collapse many imponderables into the single forecast that most of us want, but to force us to think and act to create the future as "self-fulfilling prophecy." That is, with the scenario or alternative-futures approach, the futurist projects the logical multivariate patterns or forms that growth *can* take, and poses their alternative consequences, in order to place before the decision-makers the choices that must be made if desired, rather than undesired, futures are to be realized.

This carefully reasoned approach to futurism bears heavily on the disagreement between the "Kahnites" and the "Romeites" and others on the optimistic versus pessimistic views of mankind's future. Kahn, a prime developer of the scenario approach, actually abandons his own methodology and is typically willing to collapse great areas of complexity and uncertainty into his legitimate, personal, single prediction of an optimistic future for mankind. By contrast, those adhering to Club of Rome and other views must see this as an insufferable, if not irresponsible, personal arrogance. For what they are trying to do is to arouse mankind to the very real dangers we face and to thereby force us to begin to choose our futures. From this point of view Kahn's projection of optimism, by creating an impression all these horrible things will take care of themselves or pass away, saps both leadership and popular motivation to think and act, and thereby undercuts everything they are trying to do.

Our personal feeling is that, if one takes a pluralistic, Lewinian or field theoretical view of motivation—which is the only position that makes sense to us—*both* positions are needful and socially desirable. Like Burridan's ass, we must have the carrot of hope to motivate us to better the future, which optimism encourages. But we must also be prodded by the stick of the horrendous disaster pessimism foresees if we are to reach optimism's future.

Chapter 3
THE HOLE IN THE
PREDICTION MACHINE

We have scanned the prospects for futures forecasting. Now let us focus on the main problem to which this book is addressed: the need for a futures-relevant psychology, or the problem of "the hole in the prediction machine."

With exceptions to be noted in the next chapter, predicting futures is at present overwhelmingly the domain of scientists trained in and orienting to *externality*—or forces dominantly seen as acting *upon* us, from outside, rather than acting outward from *within* us. For example, the works of de Jouvenel, Kahn, Helmer, and The Club of Rome list hundreds of participating externalists—agronomists, physicists, mathematicians, computer scientists, engineers, systems analysts, and operations researchers, and among the social sciences, economists, sociologists, political scientists, and an occasional historian. A place within the "sysem" for internality, or man's needs, is of course more or less recognized by all these specialists. But search these and other futurist works from end to end and you will be lucky to find more than one or two experts listed who were trained in the chief science of internality, psychology, which ironically is by far the largest of the social sciences in numbers of professionals. From this perspective present-day futurism often seems a cartoon of externality: the giant machine atwitter with lights and strange burblings, which spews out trends, equations, extrapolations, cost-effectiveness ratios, outcome-value arrays, S-shaped and exponential curves, minimax and Bayesian solutions, objective and subjective probability statements—while tended by two aseptically white-frocked humanoids at the "input" and "output" ends. Just as for Arthur Koestler humanism within modern psychology was the "ghost in the machine," so psychology within futurism is the "hole" in the "machine."

The precise location of this hole, and the probable function of whatever is to fill it, have not gone unnoticed. Of "subjective" aspects to futures prediction, Mesarovic notes: "Uncertainty in the analysis of the

26

future is due to the impossibility of predicting. . . all choices which will be made within the system that will influence its evolution.''[1] With "choice," of course, *the human being* enters the system. Of the impact of individual and mass psychology on the future, de Jouvenel collapses volumes into the observation: "Any power, whether social or political, is maintained by people's attitudes; any project, short or long, shallow or profound, is founded in their attitudes and behavior.''[2] Yet despite this recognition among futurists the hole still remains; there is no adequate psychology for futurism.

One could cite many reasons for this lack, but essentially most of them derive from what Herman Kahn calls "educated incapacity"—or the inability of the specialist to understand the problem, or contribute to its solution, through having been trained not to venture beyond the sacred boundaries of the partial view to attain a holistic grasp of reality. This affliction has operated in two ways to exclude formal psychology from futurism. It has worked, first, through the more external social sciences, which have already gained a foothold in futurism. Once the domain of psychologically adept masters like Max Weber, for many years now much of sociology, economics, and political science has tried to bypass or transcend the messiness of man at the psychological level. The result is a futurism that often suffers from the same problem as the idea of an immaculate conception: the suspicion of a scenario more fiction than fact. Much worse, however, are what might be termed the "ostrich" and the "minnow" effects in psychology. One is the tendency of psychologists to bury their heads in some tiny phenomenon excluding the surround that gives it meaning. The other is the way crude but useful metatheories and macrotheories have disintegrated into highly sophisticated but generally useless microtheories in psychology, like the spawning of many bewildering schools of frantic minnows by a few appreciable (but now, alas, long-departed) whales.[3]

The problem from the viewpoint of anyone external to psychology today who wants to make use of its glittering and multifaceted findings is that it is all in fragments, like the pieces of a shattered vase. Consequently, most nonpsychologists who need a psychology for some specific use, as with a vase for carrying water, turn to inadequate but still holistically serviceable old vessels like Freudianism to get the job done. Fortunately for those who wish to assemble a futures-relevant psychology from among the scraps, the insights of the potential users-—these futurists who are on the firing line, so to speak—help to identify what is needed. I look for guidance from de Jouvenel, Kahn, and the

Club of Rome scientists here and then examine the Delphi potential associated with Helmer in a later chapter.

De JOUVENEL'S PSYCHOLOGY

Earlier I remarked de Jouvenel's psychological acumen. Among the classic perspectives that have shaped psychology his orientation is closest to the Gestalt school. The correspondence is that Gestalt psychology was centered in a feeling for the individual human being, as first, the *perceiver* of himself and his surroundings as a wedded whole, and then as a thinker and actor in adapting to or shaping this perceived whole. The advantage of this orientation to futurism is that Gestalt is an imprecise psychology of relationships, as opposed to behaviorism's precise specification of parts; hence the Gestalt perspective can be used to mentally fling oneself over the great distances that the futurist task requires. In his emphasis on "Ego, the creator of the future," de Jouvenel can also be seen as extending the *self*-psychology, which is being rediscovered by contemporary psychology after a period of discomfort with the difficulty of empirically defining what was obvious to William James and Sigmund Freud.[4]

Fascinating, too, is the correspondence between de Jouvenel's concept of the functions of primary, secondary, and tertiary forecasts and social perception studies by Hadley Cantril, which underlie more recent "interpersonal perception" work in social psychology.[5] For de Jouvenel the *primary* forecast is of a less-than-ideal future. We follow with a *secondary* forecast or "fan" of several possible alternatives, or "futuribles." Taking first and second positions into mind we then project a *tertiary* forecast of the best alternative. This is much akin to the transactional theory of perception of Cantril and Adelbert Ames.[6]

De Jouvenel notes that "the future states of a system can be known if its dynamics are completely known."[7] Or again that it is "remarkable that currents strongly affecting the future are in general fairly well perceived."[8] This brings to mind the field-theoretical orientation of Kurt Lewin. The Gestalt view was of man as perceiver and cognitive processor of whole *systems* of information. Lewin extended this view to embrace the whole of our functioning, seeing each of us as perceiving, feeling, thinking, acting, continually changing whole systems ourselves, within the larger social system. Particularly notable was the rooting of Lewin's field theory in forceful visualizations of space and time.

He was possibly the first in psychology to analyze our motivations clearly in terms of the child's relation to his future as an adult and the adult as also motivated by goals lying in the future. Though scraps of Lewin's work still appear in today's textbooks, nowhere, sad to say, is the unrivaled scope of his approach taught to any appreciable degree.[9]

"A forecast is never so useful as when it warns men of a crisis, because it spurs them to prevent the event if it is masterable," de Jouvenel says. He then remarks that most experts tend to give "crisis-excluded forecasts" (e.g., Kahn's "surprise-free projections"). The reason for this is that a "crisis is abhorrent to the reasonable man" and raises "visions for which the rational mind can find no place."[10] De Jouvenel then analyzes the problem of anticipating crisis in terms of sensing *system disequilibriums*. Again we encounter a correspondence to Lewin. Both his psychology of personality and his social psychology are built around concepts of tension that disturbs and then is reduced to restore system equilibrium in both man and society.

De Jouvenel calls attention to the work of psychologist George Katona in consumer intention versus consumer attitude surveys, which seems of considerable possible consequence for an adequate futures psychology. Writing of economic forecasting, he tells of the conviction of economists James Tobin and Arthur Okun that consumer behavior can be adequately predicted by intention surveys or surveys recording what buyers say they want or wish to buy at some future point. Katona, however, who carefully studied the matter for more than two decades, presents a much more compelling case for forecasting actual consumer behavior based on questions that probe buyer attitudes rather than stated intentions.

This hoary controversy is of special interest because it applies to modern opinion polling and the development, in my last chapters, of a demonstrational psychology for futures prediction. Opinion polling today, for example, of political candidate futures, is overwhelmingly a matter of adding up intentions, who people say they prefer, and from this information then very cautiously forecasting immediate futures—that is, what would happen "if the election were held today." Why this caution? Because lack of success in true forecasting has made most pollsters wary. Yet as I shall develop in Chapter 9, it seems possible to tap into surprisingly powerful predictive currents by comparing individual voter or buyer preferences with their perception of which candidate or product will most likely be the *group* preference.

KAHN'S PSYCHOLOGY

Predictably it is out of Kahn's capacity for innovative systems thinking that many of his insights into the needs for an adequate psychology emerge. In trying to anticipate trends he remarks the importance of frustrations to rising levels of national expectations as a cause for world instability. Again this reminds me of the work of Lewin and his students in *level of aspiration*. As I suggest elsewhere, the possibilities of these and Gunnar Myrdal's "snowballing" concepts in terms of the effects on personal and social futures of upward or positive, and downward or negative, cyclings have barely been scratched by social science.[11]

Kahn boldly speculates on the phase, stage, cycles kind of system developmental phenomena, which the ancient Chinese explored with such sophistication in *I Ching,* He discusses, for example, the "modified Greek theory of political cycles," whereby aristocracy leads to oligarchy, oligarchy to democracy, democracy to anarchy, and so forth.[12] Within psychology Lewin, Lippitt, and White pioneered in experimentally investigating such cycling effects. They studied the effects of varying sequences of democratic, authoritarian, and laissez faire governing styles—another work bearing greatly on the study of futures, which has been insufficiently pursued.[13]

As *The Next 200 Years* and earlier books illuminate, Kahn predicts a possibly better balanced "Augustinian Age" lying ahead.[14] To us this underlines the need for much more research by psychologists into the implications of Abraham Maslow's well-known developmental schema. That is, the logical thrust of Maslow's defense–growth needs hierarchy is, given sufficient wealth and an adequate distribution, to project a better future for mankind through increasing psychological maturity.[15] A researchable question is this: How does this relate to the balanced state we noted earlier of J. S. Mill, Kahn, The Club of Rome, et cetera?

It is in Kahn's feeling for the sequence of large-system impact on developmental change in man, and how the resultant psychological change may in turn shape our future, that he reveals the potential for a new dialectical psychology. In other words, here is a physicist by training pointing to the predictive usefulness of tracking how "the socialization of the child, the development of character, character changes in later life" act to shape the future. Within developmental psychology Klaus Riegel,[16] Urie Bronfenbrenner,[17] and David McClelland have tackled these problems, but in relation to need and potential this work has only barely begun.

THE CLUB OF ROME PSYCHOLOGY

"Our representation of the world system development is obviously man-oriented, since on the final, highest level of the hierarchy we consider the individual's needs and concerns. This does not imply, however, that man can, or even ought to be the sole arbiter of his destiny. Indeed, his environment on whatever level—economic, ecological, or any other—can very well preempt all the choices he may try to exercise. In other words, no matter what his goals or his actions, the future might be determined solely by the inevitable internal momentum of developmental processes."[18]

In this way Mesarovic and Pestel place human action—and psychology—within a realistic framework of larger system constraints. However, within the degree of freedom open to man, varying according to situation, they are particularly eloquent on the need for attention to an area in which social psychologists have carried out a considerable body of work: the study of attitudes and (to much less extent) values from the viewpoint of changing them. As far as the "world system is concerned, drastic changes in the norm stratum—that is, in the value system and the goals of man—are necessary in order to solve energy, food, and other crises, i.e., social changes and changes in individual attitudes are needed if the transition to organic growth is to take place."[19]

This need for new concentration on the area of values change was earlier trumpeted by Dennis Meadows in *Limits to Growth*. And what is the present state of the art in psychology? Unfortunately, most social psychologists are so immersed in the minutiae of conflicting views about attitudes and attitude change that social practitioners pay them little attention.[20] Meanwhile, the one very striking work in *values* change, by Milton Rokeach, only slowly gains recognition, adherents, and needful testing.[21]

As for the concern about cooperating in social advancement: ". . .there is no more urgent task in the quest for peace than to help guide the world system onto the path of organic growth through the various stages of its evolution through cooperation rather than confrontation."[22] Beginning with the ground-breaking work of Lewin's student Morton Deutsch[23] and the classic field experiments of Muzifer Sherif,[24] and including the brilliant applied thought of Charles Osgood,[25] an exceptionally productive body of work was compiled within social psychology tailored to exactly this concern. Yet today it is viewed as "old hat" within psychology and no one is trying to apply this work to the futurist task.

Finally, to identify the largest hole in the machine—and pose another challenge to psychology—here are the requirements of the new "global ethic" Mesarovic and Pestel feel is required if mankind, that is ourselves, and our children, and their children, are to survive and realize our future.

They feel there must be developed:

1. A world consciousness—a new sense of world brotherhood.
2. A new ethic in the use of material resources.
3. An attitude toward nature based on harmony rather than conquest.
4. "If the human species is to survive, man must develop a sense of identification with future generations."[26]

Within psychology, the "grand old men" have written copiously of the need for such goals—that is, Carl Jung,[27] Erik Erikson,[28] Erich Fromm,[29] Kurt Lewin,[30] Abraham Maslow.[31] But where are the "grand young men" today to realize them in the action research terms Kurt Lewin tried to make meaningful? Have all of them had their aspirations shorn in graduate school by teachers whose historical fate it was to be forced to labor in the vineyards of ever smaller certainties? The main challenge to psychology today is to free itself from a bureaucracy of mind constraining and diverting the once-hopeful science of mind. The danger it faces is that it will provide little more than an academic sideshow, while the world's movers and shakers, faced with the need to *act* shape the future, either ignore it or make up their own psychology.

FUTURISM AND THE PSYCHOLOGY OF IDEOLOGY

An aspect in which I have a personal investment is the relation of an adequate psychology of ideology—or the nature and dialectics of left, right, and "middle" belief systems—to futures prediction. De Jouvenel first speaks to this interest by noting that among the causes of the future, "who sits up there' makes a major difference. . . and it seems foolish not to recognize that individual decisions are historical causes in their own right."[32] To make his point he describes two "great industrial countries" gripped in much the same throes of economic depression and unemployment. In the same month new leaders come to power in each country. They initiate similar economic and centralizing policies—but thereafter the two countries pursue vastly different paths, for the two leaders are Adolf Hitler and Franklin Roosevelt.

Thus de Jouvenel touches on the question of how ideological differences may radically change the future by selecting a rightist leader and a liberal leader to pose a meaningful polarity. How is it they effect change? "What is important is to find points of fulcrum on which we can exert pressure, thereby deflecting the course of events in one direction rather than another."[33] Then, in assessing the relation of political to economic forecasting, he remarks how one can "see political passions causing a diversion from the course of things that might be foreseen from social economy alone."[34] He further remarks of political factors that "to ignore them or weight them insufficiently is to condemn oneself to grave errors of judgment and forecasting.."[35]

It is, however, in his consideration of the power of ideas that de Jouvenel's observations are most directed to our interest. The future may to a significant degree derive from an "ecology of social ideas," some of which "compound with one another," while "others are at war," comprising an ecosystem with "periods of stability as well as periods of rapid change."[36] The forecasting of ideas is "of the greatest importance. . . . On the assumption that changes in society are the result of changes in ideas, we cannot forecast the former without forecasting the latter."[37]

Among futurists Herman Kahn is particularly sensitive to such changes in terms of the components and dynamics of ideology. He speaks of the confrontation of the "humanist left" of the 1960s counterculture and the emergent new conservatism of a "responsible center," which in 1972 he predicted would dominate governments of the West by 1980.[38] Characteristic of his supple use of historical analogy he relates this contemporary phenomenon to the struggle between the Guelfs and Ghibellines in Renaissance Italy. Moreover, he goes beyond most contemporary study of the psychology of ideology to begin to get at fundamental meanings in terms of dialectical thought. "We could have a situation in which, in Hegelian terms, the traditional society is the thesis, the counter-culture the antithesis, and the result of the conflict and/or combination of the two would be a new synthesis."[39]

Beneath all of this Kahn has sensed quite accurately the basic left-right ideological polarity that among psychologists Silvan Tomkins best articulates, ". . . no matter how objective one may try to be . . . most views of the future are almost necessarily founded upon some ideological preconceptions about the nature of man."[40] Kahn remarks the fundamental importance and persistence of the "Augustinian" and "Pelagian" views of man. In the fifth century St. Augustine "accused the British theologian Pelagius of the heresy of believing that man could achieve salvation through his own efforts; that is, man was basically the master of his fate and through his unaided efforts could be good. St. Augustine took the opposing view, which came to be the orthodox Christian point of view, that man was fundamentally sinful and could achieve salvation only through God's grace. In the modern world, Augustinians tend to be conservatives. The liberal tradition (including Marxism) is Pelagian."[41] To make sure no one fails to get his main point, Kahn emphasizes: "Whether we are Augustinians or Pelagians strongly affects our view of the future."[42]

Finally, Mesarovic notes of the famous "limits to growth" that there are "inner" as well as "outer" limits within man himself. "They are no less real because it is man who is ultimately the generator of change and the watchdog who keeps it from getting out of control."[43]

Thus throughout these key works of the futurists, in passages here and there, one may find recognition of the impact upon the future of the dialectics of ideology, or of right versus left personalities and groups. One also finds, however, that no adequate way of organizing these perceptions and making them useful has yet been found. This is the exemplary task for Chapters 6 through 8. Meanwhile, in the next two chapters I will examine how both the right- and the left-brain hemispheres of our minds work in futures forecasting.

Chapter 4
LEFT-BRAIN FORECASTING

Though psychology is today the laggard in futurism, this was not so at its beginning. Gustave Fechner, in creating the science of psychophysics in the mid-1800s, experimentally attacked the basic philosophical mind-body problem involved in futurism. This is the question of how our minds relate to their physical encasement within the flesh and bones of our bodies and within the social and natural surroundings we perceive and act upon through these bodies.

The founder of experimental psychology, Wilhelm Wundt, advanced on this problem with a massive Germanic attempt to define the crucial psychological variables and to project their relation to social action—or to how we may shape our bodily, natural, and social surroundings to our will. He saw man, through evolution, chiefly characterized from the lower animals by a unique information-processing and decisional system. At the input end were key processes of selective perception and attention, by which we radically narrow much matter to be dealt with to a few manageable alternatives. Then by referral to our goals—or to our concepts of desirable futures—we select preferable paths, and through *volition* try to shape our environment to our will. Without this characteristically human processing and guidance *system*, "men would forever be at the mercy of sporadic thoughts, memories, and perceptions."[2]

Simultaneously in America, the great William James was expressing essentially the same orientation to mind and the future in his formative psychology.

"We see that the mind is at every stage a theatre of simultaneous possibilities. Consciousness consists of the comparison of these with each other, the selection of some, and the suppression of others, of the rest by the reinforcing and inhibiting agency of attention . . . The mind, in short, works on the data it receives much as a sculptor works on his block of stone. . . . We may, if we like, by our reasoning unwind things back to that black and jointless continuity of space and moving clouds of swarming atoms which science calls the only real world. But all the while the world we feel and live in will be that which our ancestors and we, by slowly cumulative strokes of choice, have extricated out of this, like sculptors, by simply rejecting certain portions of the given stuff. Other sculptors, other statues from the same stone! Other minds, other worlds, from the same monotonous and inexpressive chaos!"[3]

Since these early times there has always been some body of work in psychology bearing on the future. The educational and occupational fates of most of us, for example, are today dependent on the advertised power of the psychological testing industry to predict futures: that is, how well we'll perform if allowed into college, or how well we'll manage if allowed up the next rung of the executive ladder. There also exists today a worldwide polling and marketing research industry built upon psychological and statistical studies. Within formal psychology there has also accumulated a mass of studies bearing on many aspects of futures prediction—for example, work in social interaction,[4] Baysian inference,[5] judgment under uncertainty,[6] response biases,[7] eliciting subjective probabilities,[8] dissonance and attribution theory,[9] the psychology of intuition,[10] and the Gestalt and Lewinian work we personally find most suggestive.[11]

The problem is that the potpourri of psychology has never been organized to deal with the future in the systematic way psychologists have approached most other basic human concerns. (Many ingredients make a stew, for example, but to them must be added both the desire to produce something good to eat and a knowledge of combining and timing for the heating of ingredients. The same is true for a psychology of futurism.) Thus, the modest aim for this chapter—and this book as a whole—is to try to organize a few central aspects of a vast and often bewildering subject.

To begin with the questions that earlier seized me, let us return to my wonderment at the pioneering McGregor and Cantril studies. Why did a majority of McGregor's 400 participants successfully predict the outcomes of nine out of nine social events? How did Cantril's 215 participants predict 16 out of 25? The most compelling answers seem to be these: (1) Each of us possesses an incredible innate, and learned, and generalized organic capacity, as a perceiver, feeler, and information processor, for predicting futures. (2) Central to this capacity in our consciousness is the interaction of wishes and knowledge, or "pleasure" vs. "reality." (3) Also operating are powerful processes within unconscious mind, about which more is known than is commonly believed. (4) With McGregor and Cantril's groups the results of these two levels of individual processing capacities were then refined by the seemingly mystical operation of group consensus processes, whereby vision may be pooled, and—if all works well—be sharpened, and clarified.

OUR ORGANIC CAPACITY FOR FUTURES PREDICTION

In 1960 a quietly revolutionary book appeared, which for a time helped revitalize psychology: *Plans and the Structure of Behavior*.[12] It was written by a psychological generalist and information theorist, George Miller; an experimental psychologist, Eugene Gallanter; and a physiological psychologist, Karl Pribram. Inspired by the impact of the development of the computer and systems analysis on a study of the human mind, this book swiftly recast much of psychology's mind-boggling scatter into an input-output, feedback system viewpoint emphasizing the importance of whole perceptions, or *plans,* and the structuring of behavior as a purposeful, futures-oriented activity in pursuit of such plans. Around the same time there also appeared a remarkable book by Dean Wooldridge.[13] A computer scientist who became a leading industrialist (co-founder of TRW, Thompson-Ramo-Wooldridge), Wooldridge retired early from business to become a scientist writer. In *The Machinery of the Brain,* he brought together an exciting new array of work in the operation of the human mind by physiological investigators. Examined from the systems viewpoint of computer science were Hubel and Wiesel's discovery of visual receptors, Old's finding of pleasure and pain centers, brain wave research following Berger's original discovery, Penfield's mapping of speech areas, Sperry's work in memory, and Hebb's theories of how brain functioning is organized.

By integrating a vast amount of old and new information both books began to convey something of the organic and holistic power of the human mind lost from psychology during its decades of concentrating on pieces of the whole. Then in 1972 appeared the work in this revitalizing tradition that has probably had the greatest effect in extending and integrating psychology during recent years, Robert Ornstein's *The Psychology of Consciousness*.[14] Key to this work is Ornstein's division of consciousness into two modes, one rational, one intuitive.

A perception of this division of mind functions has existed from

earliest times. Ornstein, for example, links it to the concepts of Yang
versus Yin and Creative versus Receptive in the Chinese Book of
Changes, *I Ching*. Within psychology it has been variously described as
the difference between propositional versus appositional, verbal versus
spatial, or analytic versus gestalt thinking, as well as the difference
between conscious and unconscious mind. What gives Ornstein's integration its cutting edge is the linking of these two modes of consciousness to the reassuring physicality of the two halves of our brain.

"Although each hemisphere shares the potential for many functions,
and both sides participate in most activities, in the normal person the
two hemispheres tend to specialize. The left hemisphere (connected to
the right side of the body) is predominantly involved with analytic,
logical thinking, especially in verbal and mathematical functions. Its
mode of operation is primarily linear. This hemisphere seems to process
information sequentially. This mode of operation of necessity must
underlie logical thought, since logic depends on sequence and order.
Language and mathematics, both left-hemisphere activities, also depend predominantly on linear time.

If the left hemisphere is specialized for analysis, the right hemisphere
(again, remember, connected to the left side of the body) seems
specialized for holistic mentation. Its language ability is quite limited.
This hemisphere is primarily responsible for our orientation in space,
artistic endeavor, crafts, body image, recognition of faces. It processes
information more diffusely than does the left hemisphere, and its re-
sponsibilities demand a ready integration of many inputs at once. If the
left hemisphere can be termed predominantly analytic and sequential in
its operation, then the right hemisphere is more holistic and relational,
and more simultaneous in its mode of operation."[5]

It is apparent from this passage that most formal futures forecasting,
by economists and "hard" scientists such as Helmer and the Club of
Rome group, is largely left hemispheric—or analytic, logical, ideally
capable of mathematical statement to facilitate the use of computers. As
we have seen in examining the "hole in the prediction machine," the
need for something more is recognized. However, this forces one to
enter an eerie labyrinth of the mind in which formal futurists and many
psychologists feel uncomfortable for lack of an explanatory science
compatible with their own disciplinary training. Hence, in formal forecasting the intuitive and integrative power of "right hemispheric" mind
is conveniently hidden rather than dealt with scientifically—for

science's basic function is to explain mysteries. It is unexamined within the operation of the Delphi method of using multiple mind power. More generally, it appears to be dealt with often by dressing up right brain's naked power with the acceptable left-brain clothing of numbers, figures, and words, as with Herman Kahn's or any other brilliant human forecaster's analyses.

A delight of Ornstein's book is the way it marshals many of the piecemeal findings of cognitive psychology to present an integrated picture of the information-processing flow relevant to futures prediction. This information on the functions of sensing, selective inhibition, habituation, categorizing, and brain input control through brain output is essential for an understanding of how, as Ornstein characterizes it, "ordinary consciousness" operates. Also of grounding value in the construction of an adequate psychology of futurism is his presentation of the concepts of screening and filtering associated with Bruner and others. Most important is his ingenious and empirically guided analysis of how we perceive time.

The kind of time we are dominantly aware of, Ornstein stresses, is that comfortable sense of an orderly linearity, with its clock-ticking regularity, which flows from past through present into the future. This concept of time "allows us to plan for a future, to arrange actions well in advance, to coordinate our individual and social lives with those of others. All in all, it forms an integral part of the sustaining, invisible fabric of normal life and normal consciousness. This mode of time is as much a necessary dimension of ordinary consciousness as vision is."[16]

Within each day of our lives, however, generally without even noticing it, we shift into another kind of time. This occurs with our falling asleep and thereby entering the nonlinear world of time revealed by dreams, in which present, past, and future are as one. The implications of this time sense for futurism are obviously considerable, and yet as Ornstein notes, the essential nature of both kinds of time, and how we perceive and use them, are woefully underresearched.

SCANNING AND FOCUSING

And so we've examined a portion of the wonder of the human mind. But within the perspective of the requirements for an adequate psychology of forecasting, there remains a sense of some central, vital, *part*-transcendent mechanisms missing. What could they be?

Over the many years he pondered how intelligence develops in a child, Jean Piaget found that, no matter how elaborate his theory of stages and processes became, it remained centered on the interaction of two processes: assimilation and accommodation.[17] Assimilation was the taking in of external stimuli relevant to the organism's needs and purposes; accommodation was the adjusting of the organism to this new input. From another perspective, in an attempt to simplify the proliferating maze of conditioning theory and experiments, B. F. Skinner centered his thinking about concept formation on two more interactive processes: generalization and discrimination.[18] Generalization was the detecting and aligning of similarities into "global" concepts; discrimination was the dissecting of global concepts into more finely differentiated parts. Jerome Bruner, contemplating the strategies of problem-solving, was struck by how we generally use two kinds of approaches he called scanning and focusing.[19] Lastly, at the very core of motivational theory in psychology is the view of all beings as driven by needs for both stimulus-seeking and stimulus-reducing.[20]

Beneath the diversity and specialization of meaning for these concepts there runs an underlying similarity. It seems, in the last analysis, much like the pairing of operational requirements faced by electronic and computer scientists in the theory and design of equipment for pattern detection and analysis—in machine-readable test scoring, for example, or with the machines that read the symbols on packaged goods in supermarkets for inventory control. There is, on one hand, a driving need to gather in the maximum amount of information bearing on the purpose of machine—or organism. There is, on the other hand, the need to rapidly break down this proliferation of information into manageable and intelligible parts. Most importantly, this is a *unified* process generally consisting of the alternating of these two symbiotic operations: seeking, reducing, seeking again, reducing again, in dialectic search of both imbalance and equilibrium.

The widespread use of "scanning" in computer science and its logical pairing with "focusing" suggest to us that an enlargement of Bruner's original terms be used to convey this vital pairing or processes. Let us then examine how they may relate to right and left hemispheric thinking and thereby to the use of mind in futures forecasting. It is first apparent that both halves require both operations. In rationalistic left-brain operations we "gather all relevant data" (scanning) in order to "analyze it" (focusing) by looking for similarities, differences, and convergence of information on problem-solving requirements. In intuitive right-brain operations we extend a spatially oriented kind of "feeling" to grasp the situation as a whole (scanning). This scan is then radically reduced (focusing) to form useful gestalts that may be visual diagrams or verbal metaphors.

It is also evident that in futures forecasting we draw on both halves in a number of symbiotic relationships that adequate research could reduce to types. For example, the Delphi technique (shortly to be further examined) seems to involve an initial *rational* scan, with focusing by humans employing both left- and right-brain operations—as well as by the computer acting as the prime data-reducer. The Kahn method seems to again employ an initial rational scan, with focusing manifestly by the rationalistic left-brain operation, but latently involving the intuitive right brain. We might then project an initial scanning of the unconscious, with both left and right brain subsequently focusing, as a prevailing strategy for the venturing into the unconscious we examine in the next chapter.

This has been such a concentrated "left brain" assembly of concepts that an anecdotal "right brain" gestalt might be appreciated at this point. Curiously, the most memorable demonstration I know of this vital process of scanning and focusing involved not a man but an ape. This happened while the great Gestalt theorist Wolfgang Kohler, a German, was a prisoner of the Allies on the island of Tenerife during World War I. Kohler was busying himself studying the mentality of apes.[21] In an experiment that is still, in view of the implications, spine-tingling in its drama, he discovered an ape named Sultan joining sticks together to make a tool to reach a banana outside his cage. In other words, Kohler had observed that by scanning his surroundings Sultan had identified the key pieces to his puzzle—the unjoined sticks and the desired banana. Then by focusing on the task requirement, or the distance that must be bridged by some means between his cage and the banana, Sultan arrived at the solution. However, Kohler's own mind leaped beyond this mechanistic observation. For he saw Sultan's act as evidence of the *organic capacity* of the ape to make a creative leap of insight previously thought confined to man alone. Nothing has ever been made of this discovery in relation to futures prediction that I know of, but the thrust of the Gestalt analysis within our context is this. If the ape could foresee the *future* shape of his actions—if Sultan could foresee that, ahead of the present by a minute or two, the banana that he could reach with the new tool would at last be pulled within his reach-

—this suggests by extension something profound about the human mind. It illuminates how our own much greater innate organic capacity, developed by our environment and shaped by learning, may leap ahead over vastly greater distances in space and time to foresee futures.

WISHES VERSUS KNOWLEDGE

Douglas McGregor develops this theme of our organic capacity for prediction in opening his key paper "Determinants of Prediction of Social Events." It was to him vital to convey that, in the ranging of our minds, prediction works, not as something exotic, but as an everyday—if not minute—occurrence. "Perusal of the front page of any newspaper, or observation of a discussion of current events at the dinner-table will reveal that we do not ordinarily interpret social events as momentary or isolated. We see them, instead, as meaningful links in a chain of happenings extending from the past into the future. Social phenomena are usually perceived to be changing in one direction or another, to be becoming or tending toward. Consequently, the subject asked to predict the occurrence of a social event is not faced with a task which is unusual, but with one so familiar that it is habitual."[22]

To center then on processes of mind that could be readily operationalized for research, McGregor posed the dichotomy of "wish" versus "knowledge." It is evident here how Freud's Olympian thought intrudes, for McGregor's polarity seems an updating in the future-predicting context of Freud's earlier concepts of the Id-serving pleasure principle versus the Ego-serving reality principle.[23] This is not to discount the originality of McGregor's study, for though it was carried out some time ago, it still remains one of few profound empirical studies in the psychology of futures.

His study participants, let us recall, were 400 students at Dartmouth, Bennington, and Columbia. During May of 1936 they were asked for example, to predict whether Roosevelt would be reelected in November, whether there would be a major European war within a year, whether business conditions would improve or deteriorate. The full list, with results, is included in our Appendix. They were also asked other questions to determine attitudes toward the issues involved, desires concerning outcomes, and the amount of information they possessed about political and economic affairs. This gave McGregor the data he needed to analyze the wish, knowledge, and reality relationship in futures predicting.

Wishes he saw as being closely related to attitudes; they were what one hoped the future would bring. But reality, as we all know from both sad and happy experience, is something else again. Counterposed to our wishing, then, was our cooler perception and knowledge of a transpersonal reality that might, or more often might not, coincide with our wishes. It was evident the two interacted to produce our predictions of future events, but how, in what lawful ways? He found the key lay in two additional factors, one cohering to our perception or knowledge of reality, the other to our wishes. McGregor found that, as the amount of information about the event available to us increases—that is, as stimulus ambiguity declines—we are less influenced by our wishes and more by our knowledge of the issue or event in question. Concomitantly, where there is relatively little information, our wishes are more influential in shaping our predictions. He further found that how *important* the issue is to us greatly influences our predictions. The more ego-involving the issue or event in question, the more our wishes bend whatever information is available to fit wish rather than reality.

This may not sound startling in summary, but I cannot overstress the importance of these findings in the slippery context of futurism. For in the study of the use of consciousness both the probity of McGregor's thought and his methodology are unique. Indeed, if it were a requirement that anyone wishing to operate as a futurist be forced by law to read McGregor's paper five times, much nonsense would be prevented and the field would be more solidly grounded.

McGregor also found no appreciable difference between the predictive ability of experts versus laymen in his sample—experts being defined by the *amount* of information they possessed. He found that, rather than the amount of information's determining better predictive ability, it was the nature or quality of the information possessed—or that *subset* of information on which we focus if we feel the subject is *important*. (McGregor handles importance only in terms of ego-involvement in this paper. I feel, however, a vital distinction is indicated by creativity research, which differentiates ego- from task-involvement. The general finding is that, as people become involved in a group problem-solving or "brainstorming" task, which may be greatly important, ego-involvement gives way to an ego-transcending phase wherein one may become caught up in an exhilirating sense of group mind invested in task-involvement.[24] Knowledge of this sequence may be crucial in understanding Delphi and other group processing techniques for predicting futures.)

McGregor also speculates on how personality differences could influence prediction. Optimism and pessimism, he notes, "might also be defined as tendencies toward wishful and anti-wishful thinking, respectively.[25] Both types of people tend to disregard the facts. Cautiousness is another relevant trait, which should lead to prediction of lower probabilities for events. Skepticism, or lack of it, should also influence prediction, the skeptic resisting knowledge except through personal experience, the nonskeptical tending to uncritically accept the opinions of others.

These speculations are of great personal interest because McGregor singled out personality traits that recent research directly relates to the new theory of ideology outlined in Chapter 6, which seems to have considerable potential for improving futures forecasting. The research of Silvan Tomkins, for example, has shown that liberals tend to be optimistic and nonskeptical, while conservatives tend to be pessimistic and skeptical.[26] My own research has shown cautiousness, or the obverse of risk-taking, to be a key variable in the dialectics of conservative versus liberal activism.[27]

Cantril's study further explored whether predicting the time was as easy as predicting the outcome of an event; he found that it wasn't. Among his conclusions were two bearing on themes I develop. One was that uniformity—or consensi—of predictions is dependent on the degree to which events bearing on the event in question seem to form a consistent and meaningful *pattern*. The other conclusion was that the "relevant internal frame of reference will give structure to the social stimuli and determine the prediction."[28] In other words, he found consistencies for predictions among those who had the same occupations or who shared the same dominant interests. Part of the potential power of the Ideological Matrix Prediction (IMP) system described in Chapter 6 is based on this finding of how *group* belief cohesiveness relates to futures predicting.

To conclude our examination of the influence of wishes versus knowledge, it is instructive to observe how many other works and developments relating to futures prediction or intervention tap one or the other polarity. Assessing wishes are the following: McClelland's *Achieving Society,* the classic study of the historical impact of motivation, which we examined in Chapter 1; consumer *intention* surveys[29]; most opinion polling conducted by Gallup, Yankelovich, Harris, Field, Roper, and others, particularly polling of voter preferences[30]; and new television-

–computer polling experiments, such as Choices for '76 conducted by the Regional Plan Association in the New York City area.[31] As for *knowledge,* it would be difficult to point to anything tapping this capacity by itself, but assessments of both wishes and knowledge include the following: the "State of the Nation" surveys of Watts and Free, assessing national hopes and fears;[32] projected assessments for the Social Indicators movement[33] consumer *attitude* surveys; and most notably, the Delphi and related methods of futures.forecasting.

An interesting difference in these developmental streams is the way they seem to relate to the two fundamental stances toward the future: the conservative, protective stance of *prediction,* and the activist stance of *intervention.* Wishes-oriented assessments seem to tap the interventionalist desire to *influence* the future, while assessments of both wishes and knowledge tend more to tap the predictionist desire to *sense* or read the future. Thus it seems that methods for predicting futures ideally should tap both orientations. It also underlines a weakness, which both McGregor and Cantril remark, of wish-dominated conventional polling methods for this task.

This brings us again to the central question that both the McGregor and Cantril studies raise, but for which neither finds an answer: Why were there 9 out of 9 correct predictions for McGregor's group? Why were there 16 out of 25 for Cantril's group? "It seems unlikely that this result could have been mere coincidence," McGregor remarks. "If it was not, there emerges a suggestion of great potential methodological significance for the social scientist."[34]

THE POOLING OF VISION: DELPHI METHODS

After the McGregor and Cantril studies were published they were in effect "lost" to psychology generally. They were not lost, however, to a handful of social scientists whose interests in futurism were motivated and supported by the same U.S. defense contracts with the Rand Corporation that underwrote the early work of Herman Kahn and Olaf Helmer. This group at Rand included Abraham Kaplan, Norman Dalkey, and Theodore Gordon, as well as Helmer.[35]

A third classic experiment in this stream of development was by Kaplan, Skogstad, and Girschick. It was published as "The Prediction of Social and Technological Events" in 1950 in *Public Opinion Quarterly.* To try to determine why McGregor and Cantril obtained their baffling results, the trio carried out an ingenious experiment comparing predictions by individuals with prediction following discussion in a group. They found that "predictions made by groups of people are more likely to be right than predictions made by the same individuals working alone."[36] In other words, here was experimental and statistical confirmation for the basic "McGregor effect," but they took the matter a step further to show that group prediction could be better than individual prediction. Besides its implications for futures forecasting, this finding was an important extension of earlier formative work in group processes that Kurt Lewin initiated to explore his own conviction of the superiority of democratic over authoritarian governmental styles and decision processes.[37]

A less noted finding of Kaplan, Skogstad, and Girshick was more startling, for this was possibly the first direct tap of the vein of mysticism within the idea of a "pooling of vision." They asked themselves whether "the higher success of the group is attritutable to specific effects of collective effort, or whether a certain averaging takes place that could equally be obtained by statistical combination of individual results."[38] Their conclusion was that the "data strongly indicate that the latter is the case." The details of how they arrived at this decision defy a short summary, but their finding was basically this. They found that again, as for McGregor and Cantril, if you simply centered on the answer picked by a majority of those questioned, you obtained predictions of roughly equal accuracy, whether they were obtained by group discussion, *or by computer data processing's seeking the central tendency for individual predictions*.

In other words, the two findings combined said, one, that groups could be better predictors than individuals, and two, the "secret" to group prediction lies in the data processing of individual responses.

This time the potential for a discovery was not lost. The test exploding of nuclear bombs and the U.S.–Russian cold war had unsettled the nation. Spurred on by Rand, the government became tremendously interested in the possibilities for technological and defense futures forecasting offered by this odd wedding of democratic group process research, the comforting numerology of statistics, and the new computer power. Out of this amalgam, then, was born the Delphi technique we briefly described in Chapter 2—a method characterized by the use of group processing of individual experts' opinions to arrive at potentially better predictions. During the 1950s and 1960s Delphi and its variants and extensions blossomed throughout the world of industry and government. It was (and still is) used by corporations to try to guess everything from the market potential for new razor blades to the effects of the energy crisis on corporate futures. Most of this work was applied with little attention to scholarly concerns, and hence it represents a mixed picture difficult to evaluate for successes and failures. A handful of serious investigators, however, persisted in this area, notably Norman Dalkey, who left Rand to join the UCLA Center for Computer-Based Behavioral Studies and School of Engineering, and Murray Turoff, who expanded Delphi into "conferencing" methods to link together large groups of decision-makers over vast differences via two-way telephone and television.[39]

In continuing experiments, Dalkey found the median to be the most useful index. Moreover, "where answers can be checked against reality, it is found that the median response tends to move in the direction of the true answer." He found with eight groups, of about 20 each, who were given short-range prediction questions, "satisfactory answers attained for 32 out of 40 questions."[40]

The question of the effectiveness of "group mind" was also directly attacked in another striking study by Dalkey. He administered a test of advanced intelligence, the 120-question Terman Concept Mastery Test, to 43 engineers to obtain individual IQs. He then had them proceed to arrive at a group consensus on the answers to the Terman questions by using Delphi decision stages. Comparing individual with group performances, he found that, among those with a wide range of individual scores, from 90 to 170, the group score was 160. Because this group score was close to the highest individual score, this seemed impressive evidence for the usefulness of the group decisional approach. It was his examination of those with a narrow range of scores, from 100 to 120, however, that revealed a startling new level of potential for the method. The group here was 150—or 30 IQ points higher than the highest individual score![41]

ALMANAC, REALITY, AND THE GALLUP POLL

One problem in the development of Delphi methods has been the validation of predictions.[42] Often the event predicted is so far ahead in the future that the originating interest—and funding—is long gone when the event finally does (or does not) occur. Also, the method is generally used, not to try to define the future with precision, but rather to gain a sense of how present trends can become future problems if something isn't done to change or modify them. The ''almanac'' approach was developed to overcome this problem, an illustration of which may demonstrate reasons for the fascination of this technique.

In an early study reported by Helmer,[43] 23 Rand researchers were asked to submit their answers to a list of 20 rather incredible questions—for example, ''What was the total payroll, in million dollars, of employees in the automobile industry in the United States in 1962?'' Or: ''How many divorces in thousands, were there in the United States in 1960?''

Their task was to guess the answers to these questions with no access to the facts. In other words, participants had nothing to work with but the natural analytic ability of human beings sharpened, in this instance, by training as researchers with experience in dealing with this kind of information. They went through four ''rounds'' to reach increasing agreement. That is, the results of everyone's first guess were shown to the group; then they guessed a second time on the basis of information about the group estimates. They were shown these results, guessed again, and so on. Two findings emerged of considerable import regarding the human capacity for prediction. One was that, despite the fact they had little beyond their analytic abilities to rely on—no hard facts—by *pooling their abilities* in this manner the group was able to produce estimates fairly close to the actual figures in 13 out of 20 instances. For example, they estimated the automobile industry payroll at 5000 millions; in fact it was 5828 millions. They estimated the number of divorces to be 400,000; it was actually 303,000.

The other fact of interest was the majority opinion and central tendency trends. Over the rounds the range of opinions generally narrowed to form a majority clustering, but also, curiously and most thought-provoking, the median—as the main statistic of central tendency—remained relatively unchanged. In other words, if one simply picked the exact middle opinion—50 percent above and 50 percent below—this opinion tended to be closest to the real figure and generally remained so throughout all trials. The reason we stress these findings is what they reveal of a decision-making situation's paralleling that of future prediction in that it must operate in a situation of relatively little knowledge or maximum uncertainty. Participants then showed this surprising ability to guess close enough to the truth *so that if policy decisions had to be based on these estimates alone they would not be markedly worse than if based on the actual facts.*

A criticism made of Delphi studies is that formal research in this area is overly dependent on the artificiality of such almanac methods, rather than on the rough test of reality. The effect is to render questionable this idea of the possible efficacy of a "pooling of vision." However, the files of one of the world's largest and best known polling firms, The Gallup Organization, provide some suggestive evidence for the possibility of what might be termed Delphi Writ Large.[44]

Whereas Delphi uses opinions of 20 to 30 experts and the Gallup Poll uses national samples of 1500 nonexperts, they share two fundamental similarities. One is the pooling of individual opinions to obtain measures of dispersion and central tendency for groups as a whole. The other is the following happenstance. Although the Gallup Poll customarily taps voter preferences in national elections, from 1940 to 1952 it also experimentally asked its sample to predict the future outcome of each presidential election. This move stemmed from the probing curiosity of the Poll's originator, Dr. George Gallup, a contemporary who shared McGregor and Cantril's creativity, humanism, and interest in applying social science to social needs.

Gallup dropped this approach after concluding it was a poor predictor because of the wide *quantative* margins of error in such "vox populi" predictions. In 1940 and 1944, for example, Roosevelt was the predicted winner by landslides over Willkie and Dewey, whereas the actual election results were closer. Moreover, in the famous election of 1948 when, confounding the polls, Truman barely squeaked in, Dewey was the two-to-one favorite for this experimental method. As with the Delphi almanac studies, however, the potential significance of one additional *qualitative* fact about these results makes them noteworthy. If one simply goes by the central predictive thrust, a majority of those polled correctly predicted the winner in three out of four national elections—Roosevelt in 1940 and again in 1944, and Eisenhower in 1952. It is my conviction that, if Gallup were to revive this approach—and refine it by using the IMP methodology described in Chapters 6 through 9—a rather startling increase in both quantitative and qualitative reliabilities of prediction would result.

And what has been psychology's response to group prediction studies? Unfortunately, the stream of development opened by McClelland, McGregor, Cantril, Gallup, Kaplan, and Delphi continues to be largely ignored by the field. One reason is that psychologists are understandably overimmersed in many other absorbing directions within man and society. Another reason is that this venturing requires a holistic orientation to real-life phenomena, and, as we earlier suggested, psychology is overly confined to particularism. But another reason is, quite simply, fear of the unknown. Research psychology today is a very cautious and conservative field, which ventures forth by inches into the sea of life like a small mollusk encrusted with a thick shell of protective references and peers and grants.

". . . a significant attack on some of the major problems confronting the social psychologist interested in the prediction of social events," Cantril said of McGregor's study.[45] "It seems unlikely that this result could have been mere coincidence," McGregor said—and we repeat this quote both to make sure its thrust is clear and to entice psychologists to pursue this neglected opportunity. "If it was not, there emerges a suggestion of great potential methodological significance for the social scientist."[46]

Chapter 5
RIGHT-BRAIN FORESEEING

"We are now for the first time in a position to begin seriously dealing with a psychology which can: speak of a 'transcendence' of time as we know it; encompass *a* rational mentation; use exercises for control of the 'autonomic' nervous system; develop techniques for entering a state of 'void' or no mind; and employ procedures for inducing communications which is 'paranormal' according to our ordinary conceptions of what is possible for man. Since these experiences are, by their very mode of operation, not readily accessible to causal explanation or even to linguistic exploration, many have been tempted to ignore them or even to deny their existence."[1]

Thus Robert Ornstein states the case for exploring our new awareness of right as well as left hemispheric brain function implications. Some will feel relief to be done for a bit with the "dry" rationalism of left-brain consciousness and computers. However, more will be uneasy departing from this civilized habitat to plunge into the jungle of unconsciousness. Fortunately, paths have been cleared by mighty guides. As Wundt, Lewin, McClelland, McGregor, Cantril, and Gallup clarified the relation of consciousness to futurism, so did William James, Freud, Jung, and Gardner Murphy open the trails to unconsciousness. Moreover, to a degree generally unknown, the reading of the future via unconscious mind—or the experience of *precognition*—is no longer merely a collection of colorful anecdotes for belief or skepticism. Rigorous laboratory experiments are establishing a human power that beyond all question exists, albeit highly undependable and as yet inexplicable.

THE ANECDOTAL EVIDENCE

Stories of the power of prophecy have long intrigued those with both scientific and religious interests. The Bible of Jews and Christians is, of course, rife with prophets and prophecy, notably Ezekial and Isaiah in the Old Testament and John in the New. However, both the scale of the biblical prophecies and their use as political devices to rally friends and threaten foes put most of them beyond the pale for science. An exception is the tale in Genesis of Pharaoh's dream of seven fat cows being devoured by seven lean cows. This was interpreted by one of the world's earliest futures forecasters, the slave Joseph, as indicating that seven years of plenty for Egypt would be followed by seven years of famine. (This also proved to be one of the earliest known uses of psi abilities to guide business policy. For Joseph advised the storage of grain during the fat years, not only to prepare Egypt for the lean years, but also to garner a surplus that Egypt sold to her starving neighbors.) Sigmund Freud found this tale meaningful as a demonstration of how one may unravel the imagery of "primal process" in dreams to identify the underlying rational statement. He also surmised that, like Joseph's, some dreams may actually reveal the future.[2] Jung was convinced there was something to it. He reports a case from his practice of a patient who dreamed of stepping from the summit of a mountain.[3] Jung warned him it could foretell his death while mountain climbing, but in vain. Six months later the man died exactly as in the dream.

These are two of literally thousands of what appear to be precognitive dreams that have been recorded in historical sources and in the files of modern parapsychologists. One type characteristically foretells disaster. Here a striking example is Abraham Lincoln's dream a few days prior to his assassination. "Then I heard subdued sobs, as if a number of people were weeping," he told Ward Lamon. "Before me was a catafalque, on which rested a corpse in funeral vestments. . . . 'Who is dead in the White House?' I demanded of one of the soldiers. 'The President,' was his answer. 'He was killed by an assassin.' "[4]

Another type of such dreams is of disaster's reverse—or of personal triumph or the means to great reward. An instance is the "horse race dream." On first encountering one of these tales the tendency is to laugh and forget it. But the same basic tale has emerged in so many different contexts it is hard to discount it as nothing more than a humorous novelty. In *The Probability of the Impossible,* Dr. Thelma Moss records several tales similar to the experience of a friend of hers who is a thoroughly rational school psychologist.[5] This friend, who lives on the West Coast, dreamed of a horse race. At the finish she heard the announcer call out the name of the winner "in a clear, strong voice." At breakfast the next morning she told her husband of the dream. He checked races being run that day throughout the country and, to his astonishment, found a horse by that name running in an East Coast race. The next day, on checking again, he found this horse had indeed won. The psychologist then had a series of such dreams, on the basis of which her husband placed bets. The couple won enough to buy an expensive car—but as soon as they had bought the car the dreams stopped, an ending reminiscent of the Lewinian Zeigarnik effect of a drop-off in motivation with task completion.[6]

THE EXPERIMENTAL EVIDENCE

At least five types of scientific studies of precognition have been made to date. Of all of them we must note this problem in common. A healthy skepticism is an investigative necessity in this or any other area. However, it is a serious problem in communicating results such as these, for skepticism can become so strong in the reader as to literally blind him to the factuality of the data being reported. Hence, may I invite the skeptic to receive these brief sketches with an open mind if only to gain full references to be subjected to the most rigorous tests imaginable.

The most striking of the early experimental studies of precognition was carried out by Dr. G. H. Soal, an English critic of the early work of pioneering American parapsychologist Dr. J. B. Rhine. As reported in detail by Gardner Murphy in *The Challenge of Psychical Research*, using the Rhine cards for testing extrasensory perception (ESP), Soal tested 160 subjects, including an avowed psychic Basil Shackleton, and over three years during the 1930s obtained results no better than chance. He was prepared to refute Rhine's claims when an English parapsychologist, Whately Carrington, suggested he reexamine his data looking for a *time displacement*. In his own work Carrington had discovered instances where the experimental receivers of his ESP stimuli seemed to actually anticipate the stimulus words he would randomly select from a large dictionary. That is, rather than the customary ESP testing sequence of a presentation of a stimulus symbol followed by a recorded response, some responses seemed to anticipate by a full day his random selection of the next day's stimulus word!

Soal was reluctant to take on the task, but on reexamining Shackleton's ESP data he found that, in 9800 trials, in four out of five instances, Shackleton had indeed correctly predicted the stimulus symbol yet to be selected. Intrigued by his discovery, Soal then undertook a longer series with Shackleton. Again Shackleton scored only at chance with the direct stimulus-response ESP pairing, but out of 3789 trials he correctly predicted the stimulus 1101 times—a feat against which the odds were 10^{-35} to 1. Following the publication of Soal's work, the precognition method became the preferred technique for work done at Rhine's Duke University Laboratory, where this ability was found to exist with other subjects and to operate with some consistency.

Another ingenious study was reported in 1970 by Robert Brier, a research fellow at the Rhine laboratory, who collaborated with Walter Tyminski in turning precognition to profit in gambling casinos.[8] Subjects at the Rhine laboratory who had performed well on precognition tests of the type just described were asked to concentrate on a series of roulette spins that would be made at a specified time in the future, at a specified table, in a specified casino. They were asked to record their intuitive predictions of the probable sequencing for red and for black. Then the investigators made use of a technique that seems directly related to the consensus, central tendency, or "majority vote" methodology of both the "small scale" Delphi technique and "large scale" Gallup Poll national samplings. From information theory comes the idea of intensifying a "weak signal" by repeating it and identifying it then according to the "majority vote," or whatever comes across most frequently in repeated transmissions. Using this approach Brier and Tyminski combined repeated results for each psychic subject into a single list that represented his own consensus or majority vote for the predicted red, black sequencing.

Equipped with these lists, the pair went to the specified table, in the specified casino, at the specified time. They observed, without betting, the first 25 spins. If in this initial run they observed 13 or more hits, they then bet according to the list's next 25 predictions. Despite the fact that the odds for most games favor the gambling houses, they demonstrated appreciable winnings for this method, not only for roulette, but in further studies, for craps and baccarat as well.

Probably the best known contemporary studies are those of Drs. Stanley Krippner and Montague Ullman at Maimonides Medical Center in Brooklyn.[9] While conducting their widely reported investigations of dreaming in the Maimonides Dream Laboratory they noted instances of what appeared to be precognition dreams. A subject, for example, dreamed of "Harold, whom I haven't seen for about twenty years," and then several days later saw the man. Krippner was also the recipient of a troubling letter sent from Germany by Alan Vaughan, a gifted psychic who was troubled by dreams that he felt were premonitions of the assassination of Robert Kennedy. Two days after Krippner received the letter, Kennedy was dead.

Deciding to investigate the matter experimentally, during the early 1970s Krippner and Ullman enlisted the services of the psychic Malcolm Bessent. They would select a stimulus word at random, then from it create an experience for Bessent to have the day *after* his night in their dream laboratory. That is, Bessent was asked to dream about what would be presented to him the following day. For example, one night Bessent dreamed about sky, water, and birds. The next day—with no prior knowledge of what Bessent had dreamed—Krippner randomly selected as the stimulus to be shown to Bessent a series of slides of birds on water, land, and in the air. In general Bessent did so well dreaming about future events that independent judges were able to match dreams to targets to a statistically significant degree.

Another type of experiment revealing what appears to be precognition has been conducted by Dr. Thelma Moss in her laboratory at UCLA's Neuropsychiatric Institute in Los Angeles.[10] In studying telepathy at UCLA, "transmitters" in isolation booths concentrated on stimulus pictures and sounds, to which "receivers" in another room gave their free associations. By this means the time displacement effect identified with Shackleton was more elaborately replicated. Slides of an ocean were shown and "transmitted," but the receiver reported feeling "as if I had slumped over, and then I heard songs in my head—it's called *The Summer of His Years* . . . and then I was thinking about President Kennedy." The next episode for transmission—*randomly* selected—proved to be slides showing Kennedy slumped over the following his assassination, and the song being played was indeed *The Summer of His Years*. The transmitter then projected feelings based on this material. The receiver only reported a sensation of being suddenly cold—but this proved to be the stimulus *next* randomly selected for transmission.

Some particularly important findings are those of investigators Harold Puthoff and Russell Targ. Both Puthoff and Targ are physicists, and hence they approach this area from a "hard science" background, and their work is funded through and housed within the prestigious

Stanford Research Institute. In *Mind-Reach,* they report startling success with experiments in "remote viewing"—or the ability to describe the physical surroundings of a "target" person whose exact whereabouts are unknown to the viewer at the time of the testings. The effect is of a wireless kind of "television" existing within the unconscious minds of most of us as an inbuilt but dormant organic capacity. The nature of these findings is so difficult for most to accept as to obscure Puthoff and Targ's precognition findings. After having the person being tested try to visualize the surroundings of a target person in the present time, they took the procedure a further step and asked for visualizations of where the target person would be in the near future.

You would think that surely this would prove to be an ability only at the chance level at best. The amazing finding was that, in four rigourously controlled experiments, all four produced descriptions of future settings so exact as to receive verification in a blind judging without error by three judges. The viewer, for example, saw the target person near "a black iron triangle that Hal had somehow walked into or was standing on." The triangle was "bigger than a man," and she heard a "squeak, squeak, about once a second."[11]

Five minutes *later,* Puthoff, who was acting as the target person, randomly selected one from a number of envelopes containing various destinations, opened it— and obviously with no knowledge of what the viewer in the laboratory had already reported, independently proceeded to a nearby park, in which the black iron triangle did appear in the form of the black iron structure supporting a child's swing. Spontaneously Puthoff then walked into the structure, sat in the swing, and on impulse, swung—and indeed it did produce the characteristic squeaking the viewer had earlier heard!

THE DEAN–MIHALASKY EXECUTIVE ESP STUDIES

Each of the preceding studies has impressive features, but in terms of overcoming skepticism inevitably suffers from the necessity of using original methods in unconventional settings. The most compelling series of experiments in precognition are those conducted by Douglas Dean and John Mihalasky over 10 years at the Newark College of Engineering.[12] Working in the highly conventional and receptive milieu of American business, they created a method based on approved and faultless computer science for testing what certainly appears to be a form of precognition. Their test works in the following manner. Participants are asked to predict a series of 100 numbers that will be randomly selected by a computer *after* they make their choice. Operationally this is done by having each participant keypunch his choices, 1 to 10, in each of 100 columns in three standard IBM cards. These cards are then fed into a computer programmed to (1) record the predicted sequence, (2) randomly generate a completely independent and entirely new series of 100 numbers, and (3) statistically compare the participant's earlier predicted sequence with the computer's later randomly selected sequence.

Under such circumstances, according to all known laws of physics and statistics, the third step should consistently produce a correspondence between prediction and random computation no better or worse than chance, or 10 "hits" out of 100 guesses. Instead, in studies with more than 100 groups, over a six-year period, Dean and Mihalasky found a patterning of some people who consistently predict better, and some who consistently predict worse than chance in this situation. Investigating further, they found differences in personality significantly linked to two contrasting orientations to the dimension of time.

The question of time—what it is, how it's measured—is, of course, central to the logic-defying puzzle of precognition. How can we possibly know what will happen in the future when—in terms of the linear flow we perceive as time—we simply haven't got there yet? How can we know effect before cause? Haunted by such questions, psychologist Gertrude Schmeidler felt it could be useful to find out how people perceive time in terms of metaphors.[13] Using the Knapp–Garbutt Time Metaphor Test, she found that the personality type Knapp and Garbutt characterized as Dynamic-Hasty tended to score high on precognition tests using the familiar symbol cards. Dean and Mihalasky then adapted this work to their situation to identify the contrasting orientations to time they call the Dynamic and the Oceanic. When given a choice of metaphors expressive of time, the Dynamics selected "a dashing waterfall" or "a galloping horseman" as their preference. Oceanics, by contrast, selected "a vast expanse of sky" or "a quiet motionless sea."

In keeping with the thrust of prior research, Dean and Mihalasky found that it was the Dynamics who were scoring better than chance in predicting the computer's random generation of numbers. In further studies they also found that in "real life" this type was prevalent among executives often known for an uncanny ability to make the right (i.e., profitable) decision in situations in which there were insufficient data on which to base a rational conclusion. Moreover, this type of executive seemed to make successful decisions even when it meant going contrary to the weight of evidence or logic. They prided themselves in an ability to make the right decision with nothing more to go on than a hunch or intuition.

Although relatively few social scientists have examined this work, it has, along with the Delphi technique explained in Chapter 4, been rapidly taken to heart by business and organizational management. One reason for this surprising acceptance seems to be that many of the world's most successful entrepreneurs and economic empire builders have been and are believers in and regular users of precognition in reaching successful decisions. *Executive ESP* by Dean, Mihalasky, Ostrander, and Schroeder reports dozens of anecdotes and interviews to this effect. The other reason may be the pragmatic mind-set and competitive motivation of the businessman. Relatively unconstrained by the rationalism of science that finds psi phenomena difficult to accept, he mainly applies the criterion "does it work?" Thousands of American businessmen have now personally or vicariously seen "it works" in the Dean and Mihalasky studies. And their interest is whetted by their perception of the fact that, *if* precognition exists, and *if* it can be effectively put to use, it can give the possessor of this power a considerable advantage over the competition.

DISTRIBUTION AND ACCURACY OF PRECOGNITIONS

It has been assumed that psi abilities are fairly rare (psi is the Greek letter now generally in use to designate the broad range of so-called ESP or paranormal phenomena). However, a rigorous survey by sociologist Andrew Greeley and the National Opinion Research Center has found that 58 percent of the American people report having had some kind of ESP experience during their lives, 8 percent reporting frequent experiences.[14] Of related interest, a rigorous laboratory study using conditioning methods by Dr. Barry Taff at UCLA has established that nonpsychics can be trained to achieve startling gains in psychic sensitivity.[15] Whereas neither study was of precognition per se, the apparent interrelationship of psi processes, and the evidence of the Dean and Mihalasky work, strongly suggest that precognition may not be as rare as assumed and that it may also be trainable.

The question of the accuracy of precognition is particularly relevant to our interests because of the evidence for a surprisingly high degree of accuracy for methods employing consciousness. What is the truth, then, of the vaunted claims of the psychics and astrologers, whose predictions fill the pages of *The National Enquirer* and scores of popular paperbacks? For three years Dr. Thelma Moss carefully checked such predictions to see to what extent they came to be. Only 5 percent were fulfilled, no better than chance.[16] Psychic investigator Alan Vaughan reports little success in checking predictions in much of the past anecdotal material on file.[17] Even the Central Predictions Registry in New York City, established in 1968 with the aid of Dr. Stanley Krippner, by the early 1970s had shown only 1 percent "hits" out of 3500 predictions sent in by self-avowed psychics. However, most of these hits came from a handful of people who scored *10 times higher than the average.*[18]

We earlier encountered evidence that a few rarely gifted psychics have shown high accuracy in precognition—Shackleton, for example, in the Soal experiments. Another case is that of the German actress Christine Mylius. Her uncanny ability to predict the roles she would be offered in plays and movies a year and two years in advance has been so heavily documented by Professor Hans Bender of Freiburg University as to make the gift, in this instance, seem almost routine.[19] There is also the curious instance of astronaut Edgar Mitchell's experiment, where an unforeseen delay in the lift-off time for his Apollo-14 moon rocket transformed what he had intended as an experiment in mental telepathy into a test (seemingly succesful) of precognition.[20] We noted Abraham Lincoln's precognive dream earlier; there are also instances of what appear to the adept in this area to be precognitive sensings of their own assassinations by John Kennedy and Martin Luther King.[21]

As far as accuracy of precognition is concerned, then, the picture that emerges is of an ability that is both highly unpredictable and questionable if one examines the output of large numbers of purported psychics and "lay" precognitions. The weight of evidence tends, however, to support a conclusion that for some people the ability may at times prove remarkably accurate. These "successful" or "reliable" precognitions seem to be of at least two nonrandom varieties. One variety might be termed the "gamesmanship of the adept with triviality," as with Shackleton's prejudgments. The other variety appears responsive to very strong desires or needs. Instances of preassassination precognition and the case of Catherine Mylius (motivated by job needs) suggest that this type occurs under the pressure of special circumstances or in response to intense "survival" motivation.

The Dean–Mihalasky work is of further interest as a scientific bridging of the two varieties. Their computer exercise is essentially gamesmanship with triviality. However, this game is then directly linked to personality and the motivational pressures operating within the American businessman, necessitating reliance on the hunch, the intuition, the precognition, for economic survival.

THE PROBLEM OF AN EXPLANATION

To date the skeptical scientist has offered only two explanations for this type of finding: coincidence or fraud. Both have been shown to be prevalent in the realm of ESP. However, with both the anecdotal and experimental evidence we have presented for precognition it is doubtful either of these traditional explanations applies. The statistics of the Soal, Rhine, Krippner–Ullman, Puthoff–Targ, and Dean–Mihalasky studies rule out coincidence. The credentials of investigators like Sigmund Freud, Carl Jung, Gardner Murphy—as well as the host of Nobel Prize-winning physicists and other scientists identified by Arthur Koestler in his extremely useful investigation of parapsychology—rules out fraud.[22] It further seems the height of snobbery and a lack of realism to ignore the cumulative evidence of repeated reports of exactly the same phenomena by reputable and open-minded lay observers—as if the nonacademic world was largely filled with people who had nothing better to do than to hallucinate, or to lie and risk being labeled "loony" for offering these strange reports. All this said, however, what could the explanation possibly be?

Earlier in this book I noted the social motivations providing the thrust of funding that has made it possible for social scientists to venture, bit by bit, into the problem-ridden area of highly rational futures forecasting. I noted how both the "hot" and "cold" wars of the 1940s and 1950s spurred the U.S. Defense Department investment in the futurism of Herman Kahn and Olaf Helmer via the Rand Corporation. Today it seems an inescapable conclusion that the same underlying social motivation—that is, competition between and fear of one another held by the world's two greatest powers, The United States and Russia—is slowly nudging both hard and soft science in these countries toward the answers. And why should the military leadership that funds science be interested in such "mysticism?" Because, if it is possible for men to develop what is now a rare, erratic, and obscure human capacity into a more generally reliable power for reading the minds of others and foretelling the future, *whoever gains the ascendancy in this area may dominate the world.*

This may seem farfetched to the reader first encountering such a notion. It is a conclusion, however, drawing on the surmises of Arthur Koestler and other observers of the Russian involvement with ESP.[23] As a social psychologist sensitive to political struggle, I believe this is the only explanation adequately accounting for the unusual official encouragement to the scientific investigation of ESP in Russia. Publications in parapsychology in Russia increased from 2 per year in 1958, to 35 in 1967, to 70 in 1969. This Soviet surge has, in turn, quickened the interest of many American investigators and encouraged the development of what may loosely be termed "energy field" theories of ESP.

Some of the basic notions are those that in psychology originally gripped Wolfgang Kohler and Kurt Koffka among the Gestalt thinkers—that mind consists of the flow of electrical currents shaped into tensionally meaningful patterns. The Gestaltists were animated by their perception that to psychologists as well as nonpsychologists their discipline was as yet distressingly soft, amorphous, and unlawful. It could be developed into a true science, they felt, by a translation into the concepts of physics, which had a 200-year historical lead on the social sciences.[24] Kurt Lewin then extended this same basic orientation to physics into personality and social theory. He saw man as driven, not by isolated needs identified by various handy words, but by concepts derived from physics of forces with valences acting through human beings, who were interconnected in *fields* of energy-laden social activities.[25]

In contrast to this German–American pattern of a Gestalt psychology that abortively tried to borrow from physics, the Russian direction has apparently been to move outward from physics, chemistry, and biology rather directly into a parapsychology unimpeded by Western social science's concern about "respectability." Thus, the Soviets seem to examine their findings of telepathy, telekinesis, and precognition more fearlessly, as simply factual, and then boldly venture beyond the Gestaltists and Lewin by positing an interconnection, not only of mental or social units, but also of all things, animate and inanimate, through the flow of energies in fields. The Russian biologist Victor Inyushin, for example, feels no compunction in theorizing that all living bodies have not only a physical body but also an "energy body" consisting of "bioplasma."[26] The Western scientist might sniff at this as nothing but the old religious guff about body and spirit—and refuse to either investigate or theorize.

A popular investigatory tool for the Russians and those elsewhere attuned to their work is Kirlian photography.[27] This is a method for obtaining unusual, hitherto unrecorded impressions of what appear to be currents and patterns of energy flow around fingertips, coins, and leaves placed on an electrically charged plate. It is being tested by Dr. Thelma Moss at UCLA, by Dr. William Tiller at Stanford, and others, to see if it might provide some substantiation in measurement for a theoretical view of roughly the following nature. We exist each as peculiar compactions of energy within giant fields of energy through which flow a multiplicity of currents. Within all of us to some degree, but within a few of us much more than others, there seems to exist within the depths of unconsciousness a receptivity to this energy flow. Thus, by unknown means we are linked with both our animate and inanimate surroundings via unconsciousness. The relation of conscious mind to this strange subterranean communications network seems then to be that of an occasional awareness that in some of us is like the ability to successfully bob for apples.

While Kirlian photography and "energy flow" theories are appealing to one type of investigator (and indeed do somehow "feel right"), they are unsatisfactory to those with another orientation to psi phenomena. The difference in viewpoint is that of the phenomenologically oriented, or the interested layman and the psychologist, and the noumenally oriented, or the physicist and electronics expert. Those with the hard science view tend to feel claims for the Russian work are overblown, Kirlian photography is problem-ridden, and the "energy flow" idea is a convenient but likely misleading simplication that glosses over theoretical difficulties.[28] It is particularly difficult, for example, to see how the "energy flow" idea, which could fit the conceptual problems of mental telepathy and clairvoyance, could account for the time displacement characterizing precognition. A good discussion of some of the complexities from the physicists' viewpoint is Koestler's *The Roots of Coincidence*. More specifically directed to precognition is Dean and Mihalasky's discussion of relevant theories in their chapter on time in *Executive ESP*.

Both sources present a diversity of views hard to characterize in anything but more specifics than would be appropriate here. Two integrations, however, seem noteworthy. One is Koestler's analysis of the development of the concept of synchronicity by Carl Jung and Nobel prize-winning physicist Wolfgang Pauli. The Jung–Pauli idea (radically oversimplified) was of parallel noumenal and phenomenal universes linked by simultaneously occuring events that are perceived as a clustering of coincidences in our phenomenal world. From this and other sources (e.g., wave versus particle theories of energy) Koestler develops the idea of a single universe bound together by two principles, a Self-Assertive Tendency, which maintains the integrity of units, interacting with an Integrative Tendency, which melds the units into larger forms. Although Koestler doesn't speculate about how this theory might account for precognition, it seems to us it might be inferred as in some way the "perception" by the "unit" of the imminence of some event within the larger form of which it is a part—as an ant, for example, may perceive the immensity of the anteater with no clear immediate knowledge of what this huge presence represents.

Another notable composite is Dean and Mihalasky's summary of the electromagnetic experiments and theories of physicists Paul Dirac, Charles Muses, and Puthoff and Targ of the Stanford Research Institute. The essence of their views is based on electromagnetic effects known as "advance potentials" and "precursor waves." Puthoff and Targ's "advanced potential" view is of events occurring in a way causing "shock waves" to travel back from the future into the present as well as forward from present into future. By this view we would apprehend the future by resonating to its waves, as leaves rocked along the edge of a pond by the ripples from a dropped stone.[29] Muses' "precursor wave" view is of warning or harbingering impulses moving out in advance of an actual event. Here we would apprehend the future as though by seeing the explosion of a rifle in advance of hearing the report.

Another view worth noting is that of psychic Alan Vaughan, who suggests that the "flow" of time is shaped, as Jung visualized, by archetypes within both the personal and collective unconscious. In Vaughan's view, the predictor simply senses the archetype, or "blueprint," by which he is gripped. In forecasting futures he then visualizes later stages implicit in the development, or "acting out," of the archetype.[30] As I develop further in Chapter 10, I have found this kind of pattern reading operating in my own studies of futures predicting using *conscious* mind.[31]

Still another view is that of a psychobiologist and colleague of Dr. Moss at UCLA, Dr. Barry Taff. It is Taff's contention that (1) telepathy, clairvoyance, and precognition are all aspects of a single process; (2) in ultimate reality there is no past, present, or future—everything informationally transpires at once in a multidimensionality; and (3) precognition probably operates in some way akin to holography, wherein the information is equally and simultaneously distributed throughout the entire medium, so that one may pick up information, not as a flow, but through a selectively filtered tapping of this omnipresence.[32] I further develop this interesting notion in Chapter 10.

Even if any (or all) of these views is close to the truth, obviously we are still far from any firm explanation for precognition. But at least these represent beginnings in researchable directions, hence preferable to the unscientific dead endism of simply labeling precognition as coincidence or fraud.

THE POOLING OF PROPHECY

In previous chapters I have noted the common thread running through the McGregor, Cantril, Gallup, and Delphi studies of an accuracy of prediction attained by a *pooling* of the visionary capacity of consciousness. As one might expect, such pooling has also been attempted for unconsciousness, but as yet there exists very little work of this nature. Earlier in this chapter I described the highly structured Brier–Tyminski study, which seems to have achieved its results through an ingenious method of "pooling psychism." Informal experiments at UCLA in pooling predictions by psychics have shown results promising enough to justify more structured and reportable studies.[33] Psychic Alan Vaughan has also informally explored the possibility over several years. He believes "people with prophetic talents could be trained (and) if their prophetic utterances would be encouraged and developed, each according to his own lines of interest and talents, the results being constantly checked—perhaps then by cross checking independent prophecies a somewhat dependable pattern of prophecy would emerge.."[34]

The most interesting development in this direction is an experiment by John Mihalasky wedding Delphi and psi methods for futures prediction.[35] After sitting in on Delphi sessions at Rand, Mihalasky was struck by the similarity of the "almanac" prediction situation to clairvoyance tests for psi, and of the prediction situation to precognition experiments. He then raised questions that may take a long time to answer: Is the Delphi method dominantly using conscious rationality, as its proponents assume? Or does it mainly rely on unacknowledged psi abilities? He also asked the more easily researched question: Will those with proven psi abilities do better in the Delphi situation than nonpsychic experts?

In the Delphi situation, Mihalasky reasoned, good predictors selected by psi tests should show a narrower range of predictions, and their answers should be closer to the "truth," than nonpsychic "experts." His experiment showed the prediction range was indeed narrower for the psychics and was encouraging but not conclusive regarding psychics' ability to better hit the mark.

Pitting the methods of conscious mind against those of unconsciousness could prove to be extremely productive in learning more about how both operate in futures forecasting. The enticing practical objective Mihalasky foresees, however, is pooling both types of vision. "Perhaps a melding of current forms of forecasting—academic and computerized—with intuitive, nonlogical forecasting would assist in producing a view of the general future that would be helpful for both business and political decision makers," he ventures.[36]

Part 2

ADVANCED METHODS AND THEORY OF FORECASTING

Chapter 6

IDEOLOGY AND THE
PREDICTION OF FUTURES

By this point our subject has been sufficiently skirmished to indicate the possibilities for an adequate psychology for futurism. Now I narrow our exploration to concentrate on the single, highly productive aspect of a psychology of ideology.

One reason for this pursuit is probably best clarified by returning to the seers with whom this report opened, John Quincy and Brooks and Henry Adams. A question that must engage anyone who ponders their story is why they had this strange capacity. Were they uniquely gifted with some mystic "sixth sense?" Or did they share with the rest of us certain capacities that, in their case, were tuned to a rare level of receptivity? That they were not uniquely gifted is proved by numbers of other well-known Americans who from time to time displayed a knack for prophecy. The dream in which Abraham Lincoln seems to have foreseen his own death is one vivid instance. In chapters ahead we note the forecasts of other historical figures—the seventeenth-century Quaker peddler-saint John Woolman, the abolitionist and presidential candidate of the first antislavery political party James Birney.[1] George Washington, however, seems the best "seer" to note in this regard, for his image today is of such stolid, tightlipped and rocklike stability. If George Washington could prophesy, one would be tempted to bet that stones can fly.

As James Flexner records in his classic biography, Washington, like John Quincy Adams but considerably before Adams' time, also predicted national disaster if slavery was not ended.[2] His prediction is doubly fascinating in that Washington, who was exceptionally tuned to business and profit-making, foresaw *economic* as well as moral disaster ahead. This is recorded, not only in Washington's verbal statements, but also even more forcefully, in direct economic action. Among early absorbing facts about the man that his later accomplishments have obscured was his presidency of a company to promote the building of a canal to help bring about the industrialization of Virginia. It has been assumed that profit was his sole motive. However, according to the Adamses—who passed John Adams' original intimate knowledge and reverence for the man on from generation to generation—another factor was Washington's prophetic sensitivity. Foreseeing the danger of the split between the North and South over slavery, Washington hoped to end Virginia's dependence on slavery, and thereby help end it, by means of his industrializing canal.[3]

We might then ask ourselves what characteristics these famous men had in common that might relate to futures predicting. Recent social-psychological and developmental studies suggest that two kinds of personality characteristics were involved, one general, the other specific.[4] They shared, first, in general, an exceptional morality. This appears earliest historically, and most strikingly, in John Woolman—a morality characterized by the need to identify beyond oneself with large groups of one's fellow beings. Involved is an unusual sensitivity to the plight and prospects of the larger group, which in turn seems to be closely allied, and cross-motivating, with an exceptionally wide-ranging intelligence. To this capacity, then, in the case of the political figures I've noted, who came later in our history, was added the power drive. They wanted power for themselves because, true, it was personally pleasurable. But they also wanted power to apply their wide-ranging caring and intelligence to improve the condition of large numbers of their fellow beings, in these instances all Americans.

As Chapter 10 develops, these observations of mine of the interaction of high morality, high intelligence, and high social sense in futures prediction have been strikingly confirmed by basic brain research. The general personality pattern seems to relate to the prophecies of leaders such as Washington in this way. Being sensitive to the needs of and threats to the well-being of the group, they are, like the bull in the primal herd, continually impelled to look ahead for dangers or opportunities to advance the group. This caring then provides targets for their minds, which operate as I outlined in Chapters 4 and 5. They are, first, scanning an unusual range and amount of information, and then focusing like the beam of a searchlight to cut through the mists ahead to discern the future.

The other kind of personality characteristic involved is specific, as opposed to general, in that it may differ in type from person to person. This is the aspect in man known as political ideology, or the polarity of left versus right, liberalism versus conservatism—or to go beyond abstract polarities to the dialectics of "reality," the interaction of left, middle, and right.[5] These seers I have noted were all deeply enmeshed in ideological struggle. During our nation's formative years one of many crucial functions of the conservative George Washington, for example, was to sit astride the middle as arbiter between the leftist-liberalism of Thomas Jefferson and the rightist-conservatism of Alexander Hamilton. The Adamses, who all revered Washington, tended to play the same middle role, again out of a conservative orientation. Lincoln's straddling of the ideological warfare that preceded and continued throughout the Civil War was legendary.[6]

What I surmise acted then—and also acts today—was this: Being exceptionally attuned to political currents, these seers perceived basic ideological dynamics operating beneath the surface to events, and this made it possible to further sharpen their sense of futures. They could perceive, for example, that when the tide ran with conservatism there would be relatively little advancement for things dependent on certain liberal policies. Likewise, when the tide ran with liberalism they could perceive that certain matters of management to which conservatives were sensitive would be neglected. Also, they could perceive that the interaction of right and left would likely, at certain junctures, act dialectically to bring forth new compromise policies. Further, they could perceive that dynamics such as these, by operating within the substructural "basement" of our economic, social, and educational, *as well as* political systems, would later produce "upstairs" results that they might anticipate by anywhere from a few days to many years.

THE TASK OF THEORY AND SOCIAL-PSYCHOLOGICAL DEFINITION

I hope the reader sensitive to what is at stake here, both practically and scientifically, will at this point sense a potentially significant departure. For not only does present futures prediction lack a psychology, but pinioned to such a psychology, it also lacks any *useful* theory of *change*. There are theories of change available, of course; by *useful* I mean modern theories that go beyond Hegel, Marx, and Pareto; are comprehensive *and* comprehensible; and lend themselves to the tasks of both predicting and intervening to shape the future.

Why is such theory needed? Because according to the whole thrust of Western science, we cannot be sure we actually are predicting the future unless we predict using a body of theory that predicted future events then confirmed or disconfirmed. "The overriding fact to keep in mind when evaluating the efforts of futures predictors is that there is no agreed-on, to say nothing of validated, theory of change applicable to our kind of work," Donald Michael has noted. He contends attempts to read the future to date "have yet to demonstrate that they *do* read the future . . . elaborate and complex as these methods are they are methods unsupported by a theory of change."[7]

To investigate this largely new challenge for psychology, over much of a decade I conducted a number of experimental studies and surveys designed to probe variable relationships and integrate relevant findings by hundreds of modern investigators with the prototheories of Kurt Lewin and others. The theoretical core of this work will appear in a work in progress, *The Psychology of the Middle*. The initial framework for such a useful theory, however, is outlined in my previously published *The Leadership Passion: A Psychology of Ideology*.[8] There I describe studies, not only of liberalism versus conservatism, but also of many other empirically defined variables involved in action motivated by ideology—activism, extremism, risk-taking, Machiavellianism, alienation, anomie, locus of control, the values of freedom and equality, and the dialectics of younger and older generations and of leaders and followers.

An important characteristic of these studies was their holism and realism. The customary approach to research in this area has been to separately examine liberals *or* conservatives, activists *or* inactivists, extremists *or* moderates, and so forth, and to examine such polarities only as artifacts of measurement in laboratory studies of college student volunteers. These studies, however, examined how all these variables simultaneously interact in people in real life rather than in laboratory contexts. Their scope was further broadened by using both an East Coast sample of campus political leaders and elite groups (e.g., Young Democrats and Young Republicans at Princeton) and a West Coast sample of largely older couples, husband and wives in many areas of Los Angeles, in a variety of occupations, ranging in age from 20 to over 70.

A central purpose of these studies was to see if within such a range of variables and contexts we might define the operation of some vastly simplified dynamic structure. Finding such a structure, I sensed, might greatly improve our understanding of political, economic, and more general social behavior—and thereby advance our capacity for futures prediction.

Earlier within a long stream of works (by Hegel, Marx, Pareto, Weber, Durkheim, Freud, Toynbee, Kurt Lewin, Silvan Tomkins, Muzifer Sherif, and many other noted living psychologists) I had discerned what appeared to me to be a single underlying mechanism of great fascination. It was that at the the core of all human cognitive, affective, and conative (i.e., thinking, feeling, and acting) processes we repeatedly encounter the operation of basic regulatory processes involving the formation and abiding by, or the departure from, systems of rules. These rules—investigated in literally hundreds of psychological and sociological studies—are known as *norms*. In their most basic forms they are fixed within us during our earliest years, in childhood, by our parents, and by the confrontation of our developing organism with all other external reality. They are of further fascination in that norms form the bridge between the psychology of man's internality, as reflected by attitudes and values, and the sociology of man's externality, as reflected by the multitude of roles that shape our social action. Comprehending this, my interest then centered on two fundamental kinds of personal and social relationships to norms—preserving or *maintaining* them and violating or *changing* them.

It is readily evident there is a relation between right-left ideology and these norm-relational processes. Right-conservative attitudes, values, opinions, and beliefs tend to equate with norm-maintaining, while left-liberal attitudes, values, opinions, and beliefs equate with norm-changing. So evident is this relationship that it is generally accepted without question that conservatives seek to "maintain the status quo" while the liberals "are for change." The contribution social science can make, however, is to plunge beneath this popular—and thereby uncertain—surface wisdom to seek three things to make it useful. First, social science can seek to verify these relationships beyond question. Secondly, it can identify the component variables and their lawful relationships and interactions. These two grounding tasks for the psychology of ideology are now reasonably completed. And so here we are engaged in social science's third and most vital task—to show how this new and deeper knowledge may better serve the needs of ourselves and our society.

THE FUTURE AS A GAME

To describe my findings the usual way would prove too laborious in this context. So to move quickly to the prediction task at hand I turn to an approach increasing numbers of social scientists are using in an effort to make the proliferating bits of their fields intelligible not only to the so-called layman but also to themselves.[9] My expedient will be to view ideological behavior as a vast game very much like poker, chess, go, monopoly, and so forth. The chief difference is that this game is in real life and is played, not for chips or wooden hotels or mere money, *but for the real-life stakes of personal, political, economic, and social survival.*

Within such a perspective, then, I feel that ideology may be most productively viewed as a game for the purpose of *governing* the future. This is the primary goal. The prizes, or subrewards, or subgoals are all the various forms of political, economic, and social power sought most actively by the leadership elites, but also to a lesser extent, as part of a quiet desire simply for the good life, by all of us. This game may be viewed as the search by followers as well as leaders for some hauntingly small bit of power, for a distressingly evanescent time, over our destiny, our future—to keep for a time the ageless and inevitable annihilation of men and nations at bay.

From birth on, we are all players in this game, fumbling to learn the rules, seeking our most fulfilling roles, hoping to gain some share of the prizes. Some players are more gifted and driven than others; to their lot fall the leadership roles. My studies of campus leadership elites indicate that the players known as "liberal activists" highly value equality and freedom and are ready to violate or change social norms to see these values more broadly realized. Another leading player, the "conservative activist," pursues the value of freedom but not of equality; but above all, he seeks to maintain what already exists, the sacred norms—for himself primarily, but also, functionally, for the good of all. Another leading player is the "leftist radical," who will suppress freedom to gain equality. His counterpart is the "rightist radical," who will suppress freedom to preserve inequality. In addition are the crucial roles of those in the "middle" who exist between the pressuring of left and right. We may detect middle roles of being rudderless and suasive, open to direction from right or left; of indifference and inertia, resisting the blandishments of right and left; of the mediator between right and left; of the synthesizer of their varying thoughts; of the power broker between them; of the capricious and the actively independent.

Out of the interplay with our social environment of humans who have occupied these roles, over time a vast array of rules for playing this game has emerged. And where does it all lead? We may look ahead and see that the activity of this vast real-life gameboard is a matrix of thrusts toward the future embodied in the desire of each player either to read or shape the future to serve the needs of himself, his progeny, and his primary reference groups. Hence, the liberal activist will risk to gain a future that may realize more of the human growth potential. This thrust is in keeping with the articulations of men like Karl Marx, Thomas Jefferson, and Abraham Maslow—a future requiring the necessity of disorder to attain a better order. Hence, the conservative activist will risk to gain a future that will maintain our past advancement toward realizing the human potential that has already occurred. In keeping with the views of Vilfredo Pareto and Alexander Hamilton, he will risk to maintain what is established in the present, or existed in the past, to gain a future requiring the least possible amount of transitional disorder.

To put this relation of personal psychology to group futures in another perspective, here is de Jouvenel's comparable analysis:

"Lesage once made use of a Lame Demon who unroofed houses to reveal what was going on inside. Let us suppose that this *diable boiteux* could reveal people's minds in the same way, enabling us to surprise the projects each member of society forms in his inner self. We could then apprehend, at their origin, those shoots which as they grow will deform the familiar social surface and produce swellings, fractures, and cracks. What will these changes be? How can they be foreseen? Here lies the subject that preoccupies us."[10]

IDEOLOGICAL MATRIX PREDICTION (IMP)

What do my "ideological game" and de Jouvenel's "Lame Demon" views specifically suggest for the prediction of futures?

Out of my investigation of the variables of ideology I identified three as together best accounting for the operation of norm-changing versus norm-maintaining—and thereby probably also best accounting for our sensitivity to, and action upon, the flow of events that becomes the future. The three are liberalism versus conservatism, activism versus inactivism, and extremism versus moderation. I then became convinced that a fourth, key variable in futures prediction was the tough versus tender-mindedness first proposed by William James and extensively explored through factor analysis by Hans Eysenck,[11] Raymond

Cattell,[12] and Andrew Comrey.[13] As Eysenck originally saw this personality dimension, it was the essential differentiator between leftists and rightists who were prepared to resort to violence, and liberals and conservatives who preferred milder means, to gain their ends. Tough--tender-mindedness has fallen into some disrepute among psychologists, but sociological and historical analysis convinced me this is a dimension of much greater predictive importance than solely psychological studies suggest.[14]

Sociological and historical studies then further convinced me that a fifth major dimension relevant to prediction is that of class conflict—however, not in the traditional sense. The class conflict concept is, of course, integral to much sociological analysis, deriving from the original emphasis placed by Marx on class struggle. I came to the conclusion, however, that a radical simplification based on historical and recent sociological studies is necessary.[15] Over our history, the root political dynamic for American politics has been a recurring extension of the old Jefferson–Hamilton conflict between the view of government by mass and government by elite.[16] This conflict has intensified—and through the advent of computer technology has, in fact, been transubstantiated—by the rise in our time of what many begin to see as a new class of the supereducated. Projections of this trend include Young's *Rise of the Meritocracy* and Vonnegut's *Player Piano.*[17] Not coincidental has been the burgeoning of Delphi studies to tap the opinions of this new elite. I became convinced, then, that a fifth key variable for predicting the future is the "leader-follower" or elite versus *hoi polloi* dimension.

Last of the main variables from this perspective is the generational factor. It is a curiosity that, with certain important exceptions, the varying generational impact on futures is so underexplored by social scientists in our culture. Yet it is evident to anyone seeking the wellsprings of social movement, who examines any decent span of human history, that much of the pattern of advancement, stasis, or retrogression on the social front is tied to complexities of the successions of the generations of man. The fathers may represent one thing, the sons another. Moreover, in the impact of events (e.g., the eternal wars) more on one than another, and in the waxing of one and the waning of another in terms of life span, we may glimpse dynamics on the social level somewhat like that on the mechanical level: of the acceleration or slackening of fuel injection, and the cyclical thrust of pistons pumping. Thus

I surmised that the additional perspective of age, or of the younger versus the older, is of considerable predictive importance.[18]

Let me now take up my earlier image of the future as being a *matrix* of personal and social thrusts into the unknown. We may then project a prediction system based on these six dimensions, or potential indicators, of social movement: left versus right (LR); extremism versus moderation (EM); activism versus inactivism (AI); tough- versus tender-mindedness (TT); elite versus *hoi polloi* (EH); and young versus old (YO).

And now what may constitute their meaningful dynamics? Or the components of quasi-mathematical prediction formulae?

In my studies of the operation of these dimensions in real-life groups I was struck by certain patterns that emerged whenever I compared my study participants' attitudes on key social and political issues. It is customary in social science to look for differences. Indeed, the main thrust of the research process itself and its statistical analysis is overwhelmingly toward the search for significant differences. I found such differences on a number of issues—for example, differences between liberal and conservative on issues of racism, national defense, or foreign policy. However, more generally overlooked, but in social fact equally meaningful, are the similarities among people, and this is particularly true within this context. For example, among liberals and conservatives I found a convergence of opinion on the desirability of welfare reform, on the urgency of finding remedies for environmental pollution, and on ending political corruption, and a common valuing of individual freedom and a distaste for bureaucracy, whether of big government or big business. Moreover, here I again stray upon the central fascination of the McGregor, Cantril, Helmer, and literally hundreds of contemporary Delphi studies—the finding of special predictive powers adhering to consensus analysis techniques.

We may begin to see, then, a simple but potentially powerful basic framework for analyzing the dynamics underlying, and thereby to some extent predicting, the course of events. We must look for convergence versus divergence across these polarities, with two simple mechanistic possibilities in mind:

1. Wherever we find *convergence* of opinion across polarities on the priority or desirability of social action toward remedying a particular social problem, we have identified a significant factor influencing

both the direction and the rate of advance toward the goal implied—a factor that may *accelerate* or *hasten* such movement.

2. Wherever we find *divergence* of opinion across polarities on the priority or desirability of social action toward remedying a social problem, we have identified a significant factor also influencing the direction and rate of advance, but in this case indicating the probability of *resistance* to movement.

With *convergence*, we may see the cohesive ground for the thrust of human aspiration that can make some appreciable dent or break in the resistance of prevailing system inertia or the counterforce of other events. By contrast, in the case of *divergence* we may see a state of weakness and irresolution, where little ground for the thrust of decision exists, with also the implication of many time-consuming stages of conflicts yet to be worked through, and hence an indicator of the high probability of a lack of movement in the direction in question.[19]

I also discerned another factor of predictive dynamics that seemed worth exploring. This is the ideational force that seems to adhere to whichever end of the polarity prevails. That is, it is evident that whether liberals or conservatives have more power on an issue is a key determinant of social directional thrusts. But as we examine the rest of these polar dimensions, we may note a closely related social fact. We may observe that in most cases if the prevailing edge of power adheres to one end of the polarity we see cause for change. Thus, whenever the extremes, the activists, the tough-minded, and the elite prevail, we may see in the known intensity and dedication and special knowledge and competencies of such alignments the grounds for significant action. By contrast, where the moderates, the inactivists, the tender-minded, and the *hoi polloi* prevail, we may see the grounds for either social foot-dragging and inertia, or a state of flux prior to the seizure of initiative by some combination of High Forcefuls. There are, of course, the evident exceptions, for example, the elite–*hoi polloi* alignment, wherein history repeatedly demonstrates the phenomenon of *hoi polloi* discontent instigating the rise of new elites and new elite–*hoi polloi* alignments. Moreover, the young–old alignment is a special case in itself. On the face of it, it would seem evident that the young have more to say about the future than the old because the young will be there. They will come into, while the old drop out of, power. Yet it is the old who, by primacy, lay the crucial ground for the coming power of the young. Moreover, an active "father" generation may be succeeded by an inactive ''son'' generation possibly as easily as the other way around. So here we have a dimension lacking the more simple patterning of the others. Yet still, overall, we may glimpse here possibilities for relatively simple structural dynamics that *can* be quantified and that may significantly account for what does or doesn't happen in our future.

And so I have sketched the possibilities for Ideological Matrix Prediction, or IMP for a memorable—and not unmeaningful—acronym. Whatever its eventual contribution is, IMP will have served its purpose if it lives up to the name. For the social function of its mythical namesake was, as for my IMP, to irreverently provoke new thought and useful action by disrupting the conventional mind.

The next three chapters briefly report the result of explorations with IMP over 100 years of American history, with disturbing current issues, and with trying to predict the winner of the 1976 presidential campaign—which George Gallup characterized as the most unpredictable in his four decades of experience.

Chapter 7
IMP AND THE PAST

This study takes us back into the earliest days of America, into Colonial times. Its purpose is to see if certain futures that were unknown then, but through the passage of time are known today, could have been predicted with the IMP system I have outlined. Before we step into our "time machine," however, it will be necessary to obtain some knowledge of how it works—the functions of its "knobs" and "dials," as it were.

METHODOLOGY

Let us visualize two issues of the day for which there is opinion sampling. Let us further visualize that by means of this sampling we have measured opinions on both issues of members of all groups suggested by our six polar dimensions. More specifically, we have asked them a series of questions designed to find out how desirable, versus how probable, they feel social advancement on these two issues may be. We have, in effect, asked them to extend themselves out of the present into two projectional futures that interact to become the actual future: that is, the *desirable* future and the *probable* future. These opinions are then given numbers in ways familiar to social scientists and pollsters. Let us say we are using the Likert seven-point scale format, so that for each of the groups we have an averaged score or mean ranging between 1 and 7, and for each mean a standard deviation. Then using the customary statistics for determining the significance of differences, we assign to each polarity a rating of either *convergence* or *divergence* on aspects of these issues. For example, if there is no significant difference between liberal and conservative on the issue of the need for U.S. welfare program reform, we classify their position on this issue as convergence. However, if their opinions significantly vary, we classify their positions on the issue as divergence.

Next we construct our first simple prediction matrix. To every case of convergence or divergence we assign a value of 1. The result, then, might look like Table 7.1 in the case of our two hypothetical issues.

We now have two extremes that have been quantified by simple mathematics, involving easy stages, and in such a way that we may begin to predict the probability of social movement on these issues. We see in Issue *A* a case where convergence prevails on five out of six dimensions. Not only do liberals and conservatives agree on this issue, but also there is agreement among extremes and moderates, et cetera. Subtracting the divergence score (1) from the convergence score (5) we obtain a value of 4, quantifying high social movement probability. By contrast, our matrix for Issue *B* reveals an issue on which there is a convergence of opinion only for activists and inactivists. This results in a strongly minus value that indicates little immediate prospect for movement on this issue as far as the push of human aspirations, or the cognition of social requirements, is concerned.

One could apply the same kind of matrix analysis to obtain ideational force weightings—that is, assigning values of 1 wherever the High-Force alignment (extremes, activists, etc.) or the Low-Force alignment (moderates, inactivists, etc.) prevails. Comparison values could appear as in Table 7.2.

We might then combine the results of the two matrices to obtain our prediction values, as in Table 7.3.

We see then, by this point, a relatively easy quantifying of probable futures that would give us grounds for predicting movement on Issue *A*, versus little movement or even retrogression on Issue *B*.

TABLE 7.1   A Sample Prediction Matrix

Dimensions	Issue A		Issue B	
	Convergence	Divergence	Convergence	Divergence
Left-Right *(LR)*	1	0	0	1
Extreme-Moderate *(EM)*	1	0	0	1
Active-Inactive *(AI)*	0	1	1	0
Tough Tender-minded *(TT)*	1	0	0	1
Elite-*Hoi Polloi (EH)*	1	0	0	1
Young-Old *(YO)*	1	0	0	1
	5	1	1	5
Convergence minus divergence *(C−D)*	5 − 1 = 4		1 − 5 = −4	

TABLE 7.2   Ideational-Force (IE) Analysis Matrix

Dimensions	Issue A		Issue B	
	High Force	Low Force	High Force	Low Force
Extreme-Moderate (EM)	1	0	0	1
Active-Inactive (AI)	1	0	0	1
Tough Tender-minded (TT)	1	0	0	1
Elite-Hoi Polloi (EH)	1	0	0	1
Young-Old (YO)	0	1	1	0
	4	1	1	4
High force minus low force	$4 - 1 = 3$		$1 - 4 = -3$	

TABLE 7.3   Composite Prediction Values

	Issue A	Issue B
$C-D$ score	4	-4
IF score	3	-3
Prediction value	7	-7

PREDICTING FUTURES WITHIN THE AMERICAN PAST

So far I have dealt with issues in the abstract. What happens if we apply to real life this method of analyzing past and present to predict futures? An issue in American life on which I have obtained a reasonably comprehensive historical knowledge is that of slavery. The inspiration for the IMP approach came, in fact, from the analysis of black and white American attitudes and behavior over 350 years of American history that I reported in *The Healing of a Nation*. Though I am not by training a historian, many leading American historians were kind enough to review the work before and after publication. It seemed to me their favorable comments, and the book's award-winnning status, provided me with acceptable credentials for attempting this exploratory task of analysis.[1]

After developing IMP to the point now outlined, I returned to the data of this earlier study of black and white history to compare two key periods—the pre-Revolutionary War years of Colonial America, when slavery was deeply entrenched, and the pre-Civil War period, shortly before its ending. For each period this required a careful projection of myself back into the time in question, to feel as well as think myself into probable opinion alignments for each of the key subgroups of our system, and then to assign the necessary convergence and ideational force ratings on the issue of slavery. Being dependent on a single observer covering a vast span of time, this method would be questionable for anything beyond an initial exploration. The economic feasibility of this approach, versus a near impossibility for methods of proof, seems, however, to make it an acceptable method by Herman Kahn's criterion for the "heuristic use of macro-history."[2]

Now by dealing with an actual issue a new structural requirement becomes evident. It is apparent that the heart of this approach lies in *interideological* as well as intraideological analysis. We see that the matrix is meaningful only if we first visualize the basic left–right (liberal–conservative) divergence on the issue of slavery.

Though its embodiment represented the intense feelings and sometimes violent actions of many thousands of people over 200 years, at its core the left versus right positions on slavery can be seen as a dynamic opposition of two directional statements. For slavery, the conservative goal was to maintain the status quo, or *to retain it,* whereas the liberal goal was to change the status quo, or *to end it.*

If we apply these concepts to the period of Colonial America a matrix of the type shown in Table 7.4 emerges.

We see that in the Colonial time period the loadings were massively weighted against movement toward ending slavery. On the conservative side there was an overwhelming convergence among extremes and moderates, activists and inactivists, the young and the old, and so forth on the desirability of retaining slavery. Only for the tough-versus tender-minded was there, in my opinion, mindful of the tender-minded impact of John Woolman and Anthony Benezet, any significant divergence. To this was added the weight of a dominance of High-Forcefuls for ideational force, except possibly in the case of the young versus the old, where the young, not yet possessing slaves as property and more open to liberalizing historical forces, did not generally support slavery with the same passion as their predecessors. (The significant exception beautifully illustrates both the impact of technology, and of all similar *overriding* impacts, on futures predicition. Eli Whitney's introduction of the cotton gin brought on a radical rise of interest among *sons* in slavery, where up to that point it had been declining.)

By contrast, the liberals for this period showed relatively little convergence across the five dimensions on ending slavery. The quickest

TABLE 7.4   Prediction Base Analysis Issue: Slavery. Time Period: Colonial America (1685–1776)

Conservatives (Directional Thrust = Retain Slavery)		Liberals (Directional Thrust = End Slavery)	

I. CONVERGENCE–DIVERGENCE ANALYSIS

	C	D	C	D
1. E-M	1	0	0	1
2. A-I	1	0	0	1
3. T-T	0	1	1	0
4. E-H	1	0	0	1
5. Y-O	1	0	0	1
	4	1	1	4
	C − D = 3		C − D = −3	

II. IDEATIONAL-FORCE ANALYSIS

	High	Low	High	Low
1. E-M	1	0	1	0
2. A-I	1	0	1	0
3. T-T	1	0	0	1
4. E-H	1	0	1	0
5. Y-O	0	1	1	0
	4	1	4	1
	High − Low = 3		High − Low = 3	

III. COMPOSITE RATING

C−D rating = 3	C−D rating = −3
IF rating = 3	IF rating = 3
Conservative thrust = 6	Liberal thrust = 0

indicators of this social reality are such representational figures as Jefferson, Franklin, and Washington. In many writings and actions they reflect the conflict of being caught between the pressure of democratic ideals, espoused by the extreme liberals, and the pressure of social reality, espoused by moderates. The only convergence we would assign to this period was that of both tough- and tender-minded liberals on the desirability of ending slavery. This dismal picture for those who aspired to end slavery at that time was offset to some degree by the ideational force rating. Thus, the High-Forcefuls tended to be for ending slavery, where the Low-Forcefuls remained more uncertain. Here again, however, it seems to me an exception was the dominance of the tender-minded as represented by John Woolman. Moreover, this further seems a key indicator in view of the historical transition from the tender-mindedness of Woolman in the mid-1700s to the tough-mindedness of John Brown in the mid-1800s on this issue. Overall, though, the liberal side showed little cause for optimism.

The composite ratings then clearly suggest that if an IMP Poll had been operating at the time, a prediction of slow movement toward ending slavery could have been quantified. Such predictions were actually prevalent then, but lacking quantification, a supporting scientific rationale, and a legitimized and impartial institutional source, they had neither authority nor credibility. This is not to downgrade the unaided human predictive powers, of course. I have already noted the slavery-relevant visions of the Adamses and George Washington. There is also much more forceful evidence from colonial times of the uncanny strength of man's natural predictive powers. Later history has, for example, confirmed the publicly recorded intuitions of the remarkably prophetic John Woolman, who in considerable psychological and sociological detail predicted the course of events on the issue of slavery from 50 to 250 years following his death.[3] The problem is, however, that the visions of the single seer are lonely and uncertain propositions both for the seer and for his society. They require the bolstering or legitimization of hypothetically more dependable group processing such as, all these years later, I am proposing.

Equipped with such a prediction system in Colonial America, then, I feel it possible one could have predicted that slavery would not be ended any time soon. Certainly it would not be ended—as was hoped by many who aspired to its ending, both black and white—by the Revolutionary War. However, mindful of the American cultural leftward thrust, and further viewing this as an acceleration of the slow, general, leftward, freedom-seeking direction for human history discerned by Hegel, one could predict that the grip of the slave system would progressively weaken and that it *would* be ended at some point in the American future. Thus we may glimpse within the context of this emphasis on a *man*-based prediction system its relationship to cultural factors. I am, again, obviously proposing a prediction system subject to many factors that may generally override our desires but that may also here and there significantly yield to our desires. Cultural influences, for example, vary greatly from culture to culture, situation to situation, and time period to time period. Along with technological discovery and development, social and economic system development, random disasters and happenings, and so forth, they provide the variables of Lewin's "foreign hull" accounting for the most powerful kind of variance determining the shape of the future. Yet, once again, the thrust of my concern is to fill in the missing *human* factors within these dynamics.

Now let us examine, via Table 7.5, a later period in history, Pre-Civil War America, roughly from 1840 through 1860.

We now find that, compared to the colonial period, a vast shift has occurred within all relevant dimensions of *conservative* opinion. Moreover, examining our matrix closely, we find that this massive shift among conservatives seems to derive from the softening of Low-Forcefuls on the issue and a shift of their allegiance away from the conservative High-Forcefuls toward the consolidating strength on the liberal side. That is, while the extremes hold fast to slavery, the moderates, in the middle, are pulling away.[4] Likewise, the pro-slavery activists are, if anything, more active than before, but the inactivists are dropping away. The tough-minded are beginning to talk of bloodshed and dying to maintain slavery (prefiguring the Civil War), but within themselves the tender-minded have already "sold out to the other side." The old generally remain committed to the system upon which their riches depend, but the young are opening to the possibility of another way. Where 100 years earlier convergence prevailed, now divergence prevails among these polarities. Only with conservative elite and conservative *hoi polloi* opinions would we sense that measurement would still have found the possibility of convergence's prevailing.

By contrast, on the liberal side of this scale we see the hypothetical evidence of a complete shift from the preponderance of divergence to convergence for all polarities. Moreover, on the Ideational-Force level we see another seemingly slight, but possibly greatly meaningful, shift to the unbroken weight of a consensus among High-Forcefuls.

It is of particular interest that this shift in dominance was from tender-minded to tough-minded. The history on this issue is too voluminous to adequately cover here, but I would note that one of the major opinion changes quite possibly prefiguring, and certainly integral to setting the climate for, the Civil War, occurred within the abolitionist

TABLE 7.5 Prediction Base Analysis. Issue: Slavery, Time period: Pre-Civil War America (1840–1860)

	Conservatives (Directional Thrust = Retain Slavery)		Liberals (Directional Thrust = End Slavery)	
I. CONVERGENCE–DIVERGENCE ANALYSIS				
	C	D	C	D
1. E-M	0	1	1	0
2. A-I	0	1	1	0
3. T-T	0	1	1	0
4. E-H	1	0	1	0
5. Y-O	0	1	1	0
	1	4	5	0
	C − D = −3		C − D = 5	
II. IDEATIONAL-FORCE ANALYSIS				
	High	Low	High	Low
1. E-M	1	0	1	0
2. A-I	1	0	1	0
3. T-T	1	0	1	0
4. E-H	1	0	1	0
5. Y-O	0	1	1	0
	4	1	5	0
	High − Low = 3		High − Low = 5	
III. COMPOSITE RATING				
	C − D = −3		C − E = 5	
	IF = 3		IF = 5	
	Conservative thrust = 0		Liberal thrust = 10	

movement during this time period. As detailed in *The Healing of a Nation*, this was the time of the shift from the tender-minded advocacy of the mild methods of moral persuasion and politics to the tough-minded advocacy of bloodletting and violence as a means of ending slavery.[5] This shift can be seen most dramatically within the thought of Frederic Douglass, the greatest of the black abolitionists, and within the generally well-known rise of the violent abolitionism of John Brown following the milder methods of James Birney and William Lloyd Garrison. (Further research may find that shifts on the tough–tender-minded dimension should be given special weightings—that convergence here should be given a hypothetical value of 2 rather than 1, for example. My assignment of the 1 value is only for demonstrational purposes, of course; these values could be weighted in many ways, depending on the results of an adequate testing of this matrix.)

Comparing the two results, then, one can see that, where earlier one had the basis for predicting little movement on the issue, now the situation is radically changed. It seems evident that, if such a system had been perfected and operating in pre-Civil War America, one could have predicted the ending of slavery by one means or another before much longer.

Actually such predictions *were* made, and not simply as a matter of abolitionist propaganda. James Birney, for example, in 1840 perceived the dynamics pointing toward the Civil War, which came to be in 1865, and also projected the logical alternative futures.[6] If one studies politically and morally astute figures like Birney and John Quincy Adams, who made this kind of prediction, one must again be struck by the fact they seem increasingly less "mystic," or right-brain predictive. To a great extent their predictions seem understandable in terms of left-brain or analytic predictive powers—that is, as the operation of a fairly high order of cognitive processing of information available to any reasonably open-minded perceiver of the times in relation to past and probable futures. The difference IMP, or any comparably ordered system for "left brain" analysis would have made then would have been to confirm the "true" predictions of some while failing to support the "false" predictions of others (e.g., predictions of no change by the diehards for slavery).

To consolidate these points, Table 7.6 offers one last reduction of these data to the simplest of prediction matrices.

We see here the inferential evidence that the *direction*, the *force*, and the *rate of speed* for movement on a social issue may be quantified by the tapping of such opinion dimensions at two points in history. More points would be much better, of course, but to me an impressive finding of this exercise is the possibility, when necessary, of two-point feasibility. And though my example has used two points separated by a great span of years to make its point, the logic of this approach suggests these two sampling points could be separated, not only by a century, but by a decade, or a year, or a month, or in the cases of the so-called fast-breaking issue, by a week or even a day.

TABLE 7.6   Slavery Prediction Matrix

Time Period	Conservative Thrust	Liberal Thrust	Composite Impact	Prediction
Time 1: 1685–1776	6	0	Conservative dominance	Slavery will persist
Time 2: 1840–1860	0	10	Liberal dominance	Slavery will end

This establishing of baseline points in the past, which one may join with a line graphically to project trend lines into the future, has long been routine procedure in the prediction of economic and technological futures (see de Jouvenel's *The Art of Conjecture*). It is, in fact, so well established a procedure in forecasting that it has come to be damned by "open system" futurists, such as Robert Theobald, as the shallow and rigidly misleading approach of the "extrapolationists."[7] We have found in this exercise, however, reason to go beneath the externalities, on which extrapolations are normally based, for a deeper look at some underlying social-psychological realities. We may see here a reason for the study reported in the next chapter. It tries to see if more sure currents toward the future—and the patterns to their flow—may be discerned by examining the ideological dynamics within some potential political and business leaders very much alive and responsive to the ups and downs of our own time.

Chapter 8

IMP AND THE PRESENT

During the spring of 1972 I carried out the first of several studies to seek beneath the surface to history for its base in the psychology of living human beings. This was part of a larger study with students at Princeton University that made use of an original instrument, the Princeton Social-Political Scale.[1] This measure included a nine-point scale for reporting one's own alignment to liberalism, conservatism, or "middleness"; a scale for indicating one's preferences for ideologically differing campus organizations; and the single question: *What issues do you find to be most disturbing nationally and on campus?* Respondents were asked to write down whatever occurred to them in a blank that followed this question.

By this means I gathered an expressive sampling of the main concerns of Princeton students at an evocative point in contemprary American history, early during the spring of 1972. This was immediately prior to the ending of the Viet Nam War later that spring, the climaxing of 1972 presidential campaigns during the summer, and, following the McGovern defeat that fall, the reelection of Richard Nixon for the fateful second term terminated by the Watergate disaster. Respondents included 23 extreme liberals, 23 moderate liberals, 18 moderate conservatives, and 10 extreme conservatives, for a total of 74. I then analyzed the issues that most disturbed each of these groups with a very special relationship of these Princeton students to our national future in mind.

Not only were these students drawn from within an elite institution, but the groups I worked with were elites within the elite. Since the 1700s Princeton has functioned as a prestigious training establishment for both national and international leadership elites. In keeping with this function its admissions policies are based, not only on selecting students with high grade point averages and impressive SATs, but also on demonstration of outstanding social leadership by its applicants while they are in high school. Most applicants must also be recommended by alumni who themselves have demonstrated outstanding leadership in many fields and who have personally assessed the applicant for early signs of leadership potential. My sampling was then from within the further concentration of leadership elites represented by Princeton campus organizations formed to promote specific political ideologies. This included moderate and extreme conservative groups (Young Republicans, and Undergraduates for a Stable America), and a fascinating mediating group, the Whig-Clio Debating Society.[2] Housed in a white marble replica of a Greek temple, Whig-Clio was originally formed during James Madison's years as a Princeton student, in 1765, prior to the Revolutionary War, to provide a common meeting place for left, middle, and right during the years of our nation's formation.

My analysis of the issues of greatest concern to these groups was shaped by the desire to see if any links between present ideological attitudes and possible future events could be detected. My long-range interest was to see if the collegiate concerns of these young liberal and conservative leaders-in-training might relate to the course of events over the next two decades following their graduation. The history of Princeton and its alumni made it evident that over this time span many of these young men would gain positions of great power in governmental, business, and educational institutions in the United States and throughout the world. I hoped to find support for two kinds of hypotheses of how their college beliefs might be linked to future events. In keeping with the thinking outlined in Chapter 6, my first hypothesis was that leaders and potential leaders are exceptionally sensitive to social currents that may open possibilities for gaining the power to shape the future to the advantage of themselves and the groups that they hope to lead. This is the assumption of a leadership capacity for *sensing* futures. A second hypothesis was that if they *do* achieve power, they actually can to some degree influence the future. This is the assumption of a leadership capacity for *influencing* futures. Because of the low probability of gaining funds for such an investigation—as well as the high probability of these hypotheses' not being proved or disproved during my lifetime —my interest was by necessity greater in the short-run practicalities of developing a method for entering the problem.

The customary way of tapping attitudes is with highly structured questionnaires. These are quickly and cheaply computer-processed and give useful results through sampling opinions of large numbers of people. A disadvantage is that this approach can miss much that may be revealed by simply asking a much smaller number of people a few open-ended questions and content analyzing their answers. My method was of this second type, with steps as follows. Key words, phrases, and, in some highly expressive instances, complete statements about the issues that were disturbing these students in 1972 were transferred from our questionnaire to index cards. Each index card was coded to indicate the source—whether the respondent was an extreme liberal, moderate liberal, moderate conservative, or extreme conservative. These cards were then sorted into stacks for each of the four ideological categories. Then cards were regrouped within each category, as in factor analysis, to form "clusters" of issues with a common theme.

I then explored the dynamics of ideology by examining the resultant issue clusters looking for: (1) *saliency* of issues, or the degree to which an issue cluster was of some concern to *all* groups (determined by the number of statements of concern by the groups on each issue); (2) issues in which *conflict* between right and left prevailed (determined by the degree to which liberals and conservatives expressed opposing views on the issue); (3) issues in which *consensus* among right and left prevailed (determined by the degree to which both sides seemed to be expressing much the same concern); and (4) issues to which the alignment was *"mixed"* with statements of both liberals and conservatives reflecting both conflict and consensus.

CONFLICT, CONSENSUS, AND "MIXED" ISSUES

The types of issues that were disturbing this group in the spring of 1972 are shown in Table 8.1. "War and defense" and "government as social mechanism" were issues on which there was clear right versus left *conflict*. On "crime and violence," "environment," "governmental power," and "taxes" there was an appreciable right–left *consensus*. On issues of "foreign policy," "the political system and its leadership," and "race" we found a *mixture* of conflict and consensus. *Saliency* of issues for each ideology is indicated by the percentages shown in Table 8.1, which were computed by dividing the number of expressions of concern on an issue by the total number of respondents in the indicated category.

By this means we may see that *conflict issues* had approximately the same saliency for both liberals and conservatives. We confront a surprise to stereotypical thinking, however, with *consensus issues*. We see that, in the spring of 1972, contrary to the prevailing stereotype of law

TABLE 8.1 A Rank Ordering of Conflict, Consensus, and Mixed Issues: Spring, 1972

	Percentage of Concern	
Type of Issue	Liberal	Conservative
I. Conflict issues		
War and defense	0.54	0.57
Government as social mechanism	0.22	0.29
II. Consensus issues		
Crime and violence	0.26	0.53
Environment	0.39	0.36
Governmental power	0.11	0.18
Taxes	0.08	0.14
III. Mixed issues		
Foreign policy	0.59	1.18
Political system and leadership	0.46	0.82
Race	0.54	0.36

Note: Number of respondents per category were: liberals, 46 (extremes, 23; moderates, 23); conservatives, 28 (extremes, 10; moderates, 18). Percentages on Tables 8.1–8.4 are the number of expressions per issue per category divided by the number of respondents in the category. Since some respondents expressed more than one concern regarding the category, this results in a few percentages larger than 1.00. This looks peculiar but is a better indicator than the number of expressions per category divided by total number of expressions per category, which would result in all percentages less than 1.00 but would distort findings because of inequal Ns.

and order as strictly a conservative issue, among these embryonic leadership elites both liberals and conservatives were greatly concerned about crime and violence. The environmental issue, or concern about pollution, second highest in saliency for this category, shows even more consensus. Consensus on the governmental power issue, shortly to be defined in detail, was to prove of exceptional interest in the 1976 presidential election. I also found both wings joining in the age-old disgruntlement, which seems to transcend ideological differences, about taxes.

The three *mixed issues* toward which this sample indicated both consensus and conflict can be understood only in terms of the next set of tables, which detail specific subgroup similarities and differences. We can see by the percentages, however, that, with the exception of "war and defense," the "mixed" issues were those of greatest concern to the group as a whole during spring 1972. Highest in salience for all groups was "foreign policy"—likely because of Princeton's function as a training center for careerists in the U.S. State Department, the United Nations, and multinational corporations. Second highest in salience was the issue of the U.S. "political system and leadership." As we shall shortly examine in detail, this seems to reflect mounting concern among conservatives as well as liberals about the ambiguities of the Nixon Administration over two years before the Watergate exposure. The "race" issue reflects the greater concern among liberals that one might expect, but as Table C.2 reveals, there was also a significant area of consensus.

SPRING 1972 ISSUE SPECIFICS

Another format for summarizing findings using this type of approach is shown in Tables D.1, D.2, and D.3 in Appendix D. This placement seems wisest as a means of providing those interested in the full details with this information, while for most readers the following summary will probably suffice.

Conflict Issues.   Among issues of this type (Table D.1) the responses of these groups were quite stereotypical. Where liberals expressed flat statements of concern about the Viet Nam War, conservatives seemed more disturbed by liberals' "exploitation of the war issue" and their call for an immediate withdrawal of U.S. forces than by the war's grim human actualities. In defense, liberals wanted less military spending and were *against* the ROTC; conservatives wanted more military spending and were *for* the ROTC. Likewise, the expressions on "government as a social mechanism" were stereotypical. Liberals were concerned by the government's lack of response to human needs; conservatives were concerned by too much "paternalism" and wanted to see more attention paid to the needs of the industrial machine.

Consensus Issues.   With issues of this type (Table D.2) striking similarities in the feelings of both liberals and conservatives began to emerge. This was first evident with "crime and violence." Contrary to stereotype, it was a liberal who noted quite specifically the need for law and order. As for the conservatives, their expressions of concern about the "lack of discipline," "weakening of rules," "tearing down of standards," and "ineffectiveness of prisons" are of great interest in bearing out a key hypothesis for our method of futures prediction: the characteristic concern of conservatives with *maintaining the prevailing norms*.

"Environment" responses contained even more unanimity across both ideological wings. Moreover, I encountered an interesting flagellation of business as polluter by moderate conservatives, who by category were dominantly business career-oriented. With the same results from a much larger number of people one might predict an increasing sensitivity to the environment issue—and thereby higher internal priorities for industrial reform—as these youngsters enter the ranks of business leadership and gain increasing executive power. Television was also viewed as a pollutant by both right and left, although for different reasons. To the liberals the problem was "banal cultural fare"; to conservatives it was "TV news bias."

Despite the small numbers of people involved, the left–right consensus on "governmental power" was of exceptional interest. Prior to the late 1960s a stereotypical difference between liberal and conservative with considerable research backup was that conservatives were against, and liberals for big government. A highly significant expression of the hippy, radical, and "flower children" liberal movements of the 1960s, however, was a distrust of big government as fierce as that held by conservatives. Thus, by the early 1970s there was this evidence of the fear of both left and right of governmental encroachment upon personal freedom.

On the tax issue consensus, there was little to comment on beyond the obvious: that this finding in the spring of 1972, among leaders-to-be, was in keeping with a widespread social consensus on the need for tax reform.

Mixed Issues.   Of issues of this type (Table D.3), an exceptionally high degree of concern about foreign policy among extreme and moderate conservatives and extreme liberals to some degree probably reflected concern about the Viet Nam War lying behind a flat statement of "foreign policy" as a major concern. We assigned this issue to the *mixed* category because there was an apparent consensus on the importance of foreign policy as a national concern. However, within the few articulated statements I had to go by, one could detect a familiar left-–right difference that might be characterized as the difference between the "soft," live-and-let-live, liberal view of the need for disengagement from the world policeman role and the "hard," never-say-die, conservative view that there must be no knuckling under to the communist advance.

The issue provoking by far the greatest range and intensity of feeling was the cluster I have classified as "the political system and leadership" (Table D.2). I found this outpouring to be manageable if it was further subdivided into categories of "general dissatisfaction with the system and its leadership," "polarization within the system," and the issue of "Richard Nixon as president."

A scanning of *general dissatisfaction* for liberals indicated that within this category probably lay much unlabeled discontent, not only with the Nixon Administration, but also with the Johnson Administration that preceded it, and with the operation of the American political system generally. Otherwise, the liberal dissatisfactions noted were all familiar—for example, dissatisfaction with misinformation by political leadership, actions that ignore causes of real problems. The only surprise was the lack of any expressions of dissatisfaction by conservatives. This probably reflected the situation in 1972 of the liberals as political "outs" on the attack and conservatives as "ins" who must defend the system.

While some left–right differences could be detected on the *polarization* subissue, the central tendency was of a consensus between left and right on the *undesirability* of the very polarizing that, in stereotype, they are held to represent. This seems of considerable possible interest in suggesting the operation of a governing sense of balance transcending liberal–conservative differences. That is, sociological theory from Pareto through Parsons has repeatedly ariculated a system of mechanisms to maintain social equilibrium.[3] Within the context of this consideration of how right versus left ideology may influence the governing of our futures, such equilibrium theories suggest the operation of inbuilt social regulators that modify the tendency to extremes whenever things seem to be getting out of hand—or whenever the debate or action ranges beyond the periphery of a largely unspoken "gentlemen's agreement" between liberal and conservative about the legitimate arena for conflict. One thinks of the liberal abhorrence of radical left bombings, which destroyed both life and property in the 1960s, or of the conservative abhorrence of Nixon and Watergate excesses of the 1970s, as violating this agreement and bringing on left–right consensus where before there was conflict.

Finally, there was a highly revealing dissatisfaction with the Nixon Administration. It should be kept in mind this sampling was in the spring of the year in which Nixon was reelected, *well over two years before the Watergate revelations and his resignation.* Two moderate conservatives felt sufficient loyalty to "their President" to consider his reelection to be an issue of major concern. However, it was another moderate conservative, rather than a liberal, who expressed disillusion in terms of the specifics of the ITT and Carswell cases; extreme conservatives were to a man against his policies; and to the moderate liberals he was the expected anathema. Particularly haunting were statements we have quoted in their entirety in Table D.3—of a young moderate liberal, who feared that not within his lifetime would he again see a U.S. president whom he could trust, and of a young moderate conservative, who saw no hope whatsoever for political leadership, only Christian salvation offering anything for the future. It was no coincidence, in my estimation, that trust became the major issue in 1976, and the two most interesting new presidential candidates to emerge were both heavily identified with religion, the revivalist Jimmy Carter and the exseminarian Jerry Brown.

Last of the mixed issues was race. There was left–right conflict on the use of busing to integrate schools, the rate of progress on Civil Rights, college admittance policies for blacks, and the use of laws generally to force integration. However, there was also a marked consensus on the dangers and undesirability of racial polarization.

COMPARISON OF 1972 ELITE CONCERNS WITH 1976 GENERAL REALITIES

Let us now examine the extent to which the IMP system might have been used to successfully analyze these 1972 data to predict events during the years to and including the American bicentennial election year of 1976. This is, of course, only a partial IMP analysis, for I gathered data only for the *LR* and *EM* dimensions. I restate my hypothesized rules to aid the comparison.

For *conflict analysis,* the hypothesis is: In the case of *divergence* we see a state of weakness and irresolution, where little ground for the thrust of decision exists, with the implication of many time-consuming stages of conflict yet to be worked through. Thus, wherever we find divergence of opinion across polarities on the desirability of action remedying a particular political, economic, and/or social problem, we have identified a factor negatively influencing the direction and rate of advance toward the goal implied—that is, a factor indicating resistances decelerating, blocking, or retarding movement.

In the spring of 1972, I found such left–right *conflict* on the issues of the Viet Nam War and national defense, on government as a social mechanism, on the need for maintaining the U.S. role as "world policemen," on spending governmental funds for the "needs of people" versus "needs of the industrial machine," and on the issue of using laws and busing to force racial integration. What may we then discern from the highly useful perspective of 1976 U.S. presidential campaigns, which by the nature of politics were designed to focus attention on unmet social needs and persisting issues?

Contrary to my hypothesis that conflict issues indicate a blocking or deceleration of movement, the Viet Nam War was resolved within a few weeks after my 1972 survey. In this case, I would posit the obvious—that personal and social aspirations are continually being overridden by a social, cultural, economic system operating as a transpersonal "machine" with a life and timetable of its own. After accounting for this exception with the nonpsychological explanation, however, my hypothesis that the psychology of the present may both sense and determine futures is largely confirmed. Despite evidence of the national weariness of controversy and the desire to evade further conflict, by the mid-1970s left and right were still polarized and there had been little further discernible social advance on the other conflict issues I identified.

On the proper amount to be spent on national defense, there was highly vocal division not only between Democrats and Republicans but also between liberal and conservative of both parties. In the 1976 campaign the "hawk" positions of presidential candidates George Wallace and Henry Jackson versus the "dove" positions of Morris Udall and Fred Harris contained no surprise. But startling indeed was the vehemence with which this issue swept the Republicans, with Ronald Reagan out to "outhawk" incumbent president Gerald Ford—and thereby nearly gaining the candidacy. Particularly notable was Reagan's revival of the idea the United States should act as world policeman ("Let's make America number one again"), a conflict issue that curiously Richard Nixon had tried to defuse. On the nature of government as servant of the people versus servant of property, the gulf between opinions and alliances also remained deep and wide. While Humphrey, Udall, and Harris were vociferously signaling their concern for people, Ford and Reagan were as vocally, albeit covertly, reassuring property it would not be further violated. As for the conflict issue of racial integration, overall it did not figure as prominently in the campaign as it might have, but likely more meaningful was the fact that for the time being integration was fairly well checked as a social movement.

Overall, it seems fair to conclude that my identifying of conflict issues among campus political elites in 1972 shows some relation to continuing division and lack of resolution in 1976, with some support for my hypothesis in three out of four test issues.

For *consensus analysis,* the hypothesis is: With *convergence* we see grounds for the thrust of human aspiration, given power through consensus and social cohesion, to make some appreciable break in the wall of resistances, prevailing inertia, or the counterforce of other events. Thus, wherever we find convergence of opinion across polarities on the desirability of action remedying a particular political, economic, or social problem, we have identified a factor positively influencing both the direction and the rate of advance toward the goal implied—that is, a factor accelerating or hastening such movement.

In 1972 I found left–right consensus on the need to check crime and violence, to save our environment, to reform tax policy, and to deal more effectively with the threat of governmental encroachment on individual freedom. After 1972 and during the 1976 presidential campaign these four issue complexes swelled to the boil in fascinating ways. Not only did they provide some support for my hypothesis that consensus across polarities hastens social movement, but they also revealed at least one major way by which social consensi are crystallized. This was the detection and use of consensus issues by leading presidential candidates to strengthen their appeals and gain for themselves the widest possible constituencies.

Crime and Violence.   Left–right consensus on the need for remedies no doubt increased between 1972 and 1976, but there was little evidence of improvement in the situation. This is probably a good example of a situation presenting such obdurate external realities that massed desire had relatively little effect. During this time period crime and violence was a big issue in local politics, accounting for the election of officials like Philadelphia Mayor Frank Rizzo, and encouraging increased expenditures for law enforcement, which may have at least helped somewhat to stem the tide. Curiously, little was made of this issue in the presidential primaries. In sum, there seems some support for my hypothesis on the local level, though little on the national level. (In retrospect, this seems the first of several key instances where the Ford administration, which was briefly the gatekeeper for action or inaction on crime on the national level, failed to sense and play to this vital consensus issue and thereby gain some fervent loyalties.)

Environmental Preservation. As with crime and violence, left--right consensus on this issue accounted for considerable movement locally. Possibly the most important movement was within industrial leadership, which pressed for—and whenever successful, widely publicized—the theme of good citizenship and the idea of cleaning up one's own house. Publicly the mounting power of environmentalists was expressed in such remarkable moves as the California referendum to either block or shackle the multimillion-dollar nuclear power industry. The national campaign issue patterning was particularly interesting. The major environmentalist candidate, Morris Udall, was the sole avowed liberal candidate to survive most of the primaries. The strong stance against strip-mining and the generally pro-environmentalist position taken by Jimmy Carter also seem to be the first of these issues evidencing his strong feeling for the consensus issues. And again I find an instance in which the Ford administration not only failed to grasp the importance of this issue, but actually, through such moves as the Ford veto of the strip-mining bill, became identified as anti-environmentalist. In sum, I find seemingly strong support for my hypothesis.

Need for Tax Reform. This was a strange issue. Despite the Watergate evidence of the IRS abuse of power, no really effective tax reform was launched. The consensus seemed to have been sensed by and sparked the abortive presidential aspirations of U.S. Representative Wilbur Mills. For a time it also fueled the campaign of 1976 candidate Fred Harris. But again the pattern of greatest interest is Carter's strong espousal of tax reform in the primaries, in contrast to the Ford administration's earlier failure to capitalize on this issue. In sum, I find more apparent support for my hypothesis—although effects remained largely dependent on what would happen in the presidency and congress 1976–1980.

Governmental Encroachment on Individual Freedom.   Of the major consensus issues identified among the Princeton elites in 1972, this was the one to which 1976 presidential candidates proved to be most sensitive. Beginning with George Wallace (who later claimed the others had "stolen" his issues), the feeling against big government expressed by both left and right at Princeton was sensed and handled as a major issue by both Harris on the left and Reagan on the right. Most notably, big governmental reform was possibly Carter's most characterizing issue, being backed with the legitimization of his record as a governmental reformer in Georgia. This was also the one consensus issue on which Ford attempted to take a forceful position. Notable also was the fact that both Humphrey and Jackson attempted during the primaries to take the counter position, *for* big government, with no success whatsoever. In sum, I find what appears to be strong support for my hypothesis- —although again with effects dependent on presidential and congressional action 1976–1980.

The category of *mixed issues* is hardest both to define and identify. My hypothesis was: Wherever we find a *mixture* of convergence and divergence on an issue, we may have identified a state of flux useful in indicating the possibility of either progression or retrogression on the issue. Though categorized as "mixed issues," the following were dominantly consensual, and so in analysis this weighting should be kept in mind.

Foreign Policy as an Issue.   Until well into the 1976 primaries this appeared to be the least forceful of issues. Then with a bewildering suddenness befitting a mixed or ambiguous issue, assuming the latency to move either way, Ronald Reagan made it a major issue in the primaries, proceeding to drub the Ford administration mercilessly (and effectively) with the contention Ford and Secretary Kissinger were selling out to the Russians and giving away the Panama Canal to "Castro's pals." In sum, this issue is difficult to assess one way or the other, and hence seems to support my prior judgement of its mixed nature.

Dangers and Undesirability of Polarization.   Of the mixed issues, this was the most interesting. After 1972 not only was there a progressive disappearance from American life of any saliency for protest events or movements of the 1960s type, but also the trend for politics was away from the "ideologue" style of the earlier Goldwater, Reagan, or McGovern type to the notably dispassionate styles of California Governor Jerry Brown, Jimmy Carter, and other politicians of a new "cool" type. The 1976 campaign then began with President Ford's both apparently sensing and, through policies of passivity and inaction, fairly successfully catering to a strong national need for no "rocking of the boat." However, Reagan's entry as a spoiler, needing conflict and polarizing to gain attention and overcome the tremendous advantages of an incumbent president, made Ford's stance appear increasingly bland and ineffectual. This forced both Ford and the Republican party into the unpalatable—and potentially disastrous—arena of conflict and polarization. Meanwhile the unknown newcomer Carter, who successfully convinced even the skeptics of his religious sincerity, generally radiated the peace and goodwill toward men called for by this consensual public need and swept the country in the primaries. In sum, I find more seemingly strong support for my hypothesis.

Dissatisfaction with Nixon.   In retrospect the Princeton elite's near-consensus on the undesirability of Nixon in 1972 seems to possibly reflect a sensing of the doubts and dissatisfactions of older, established leadership elites, as well as their own cohort. Thus, despite tremendous pressures within the system to cover up and try to ignore the national embarrassment of a felon in the White House, there was sufficient left–right consensus for a backstage, as well as onstage, banding together to expel the tainted Nixonians. In view of the fact our survey was taken in advance of Nixon's landslide victory in 1972, while to most Americans he still appeared both impregnable and shallowly desirable, this consensual, albeit fluid, dissatisfaction again seems to offer some support for my hypothesis.

THE TALLY SHEET

On comparing the findings with my hypotheses it appears that:

1. The conflict-retarding hypothesis, with two test issues, is to some extent supported in both instances by 1976 realities.

2. The consensus-accelerating hypothesis, with four test issues, receives reasonably good support in two cases, with less clear-cut support for the other two.
3. The mixed-fluidity hypothesis, with three so-called test issues, is actually not testable, for any 1976 issue position or result could fit the hypothesis.

Overall, it seems reasonable to conclude that despite the impressionism and imprecision of this first exploration there were definitely links between the issue perceptions and resonations of the Princeton elites in 1972 and 1976 social-political realities. It is also evident that to determine the precise nature of these links would require much research over many years. In the meantime, we must proceed with what reason tells us are the most sensible possibilities:

1. The Princeton elites personally influenced the test events.
2. They did not personally influence the test events but rather reflected the concerns of their generational and elite cohort in other campuses across the nation. (This generational cohort, in turn, reflected an assessment of the social-political possibilities of the immediate future from the perspective of their basic reference groups and the older established leaders and leadership elites with whom they identified, who *did* manage either to influence events or to shape their actions effectively to prevailing currents.)
3. The 1972–1976 correspondence represents a combination of sensing and influencing events by Princeton elites and campus cohorts.

Because insufficient time had passed for these elites or their cohorts to gain the power to influence events, explanations one and three do not logically apply, leaving us the second possibility to generate the following testable thoughts:

1. There were no links in "truth," only random happenstance, and, on my part, only an adroit *ex post facto* interpretation.
2. The Princeton elites were both a creative part of forming and of sensing and expressing the concerns of their cohorts, who in turn—as I suggest above—sensed the concerns of the older established leaders and leadership elites with which they identified, who in turn were themselves influencing and/or sensing the flow to events.

I leave it to the reader to judge for himself or herself whether there is nothing more here than adroit *ex post facto* analysis. I can only state my own conviction that the truth—which other investigators must ascertain—lies in my second explanation.

My next chapter moves on to complete my use of the 1976 presidential election as a data base with an exploration of the dynamics of preferring and predicting presidents.

Chapter 9

IMP AND THE FUTURE

Being exactly 200 years after the founding of the nation in 1776, the 1976 presidential campaign seemed an ideal time to launch IMP on its maiden voyage in predicting futures before rather than after the fact. As January 1976 approached, the political sea seemed not only calm but safe to the point of boredom. There was no discernible enthusiasm for another four years of President Ford, to be sure, but other than doubtful factional swirls for Wallace and Reagan, there was no enthusiasm for anybody. The national climate seemed to be composed of part apathy, part weariness of political scandals and the horrendous problems of our times, and part a desire to be left alone. It was as though if the election could have been held without them, or delayed for a better year, the American people would have been greatly relieved.

It was into this deceptive calm, little knowing what tempests lay ahead ("volatile, surprising, a kind of Loch Ness," *Time* was to call the primaries by late May) that I set forth in my frail patchwork vessel. Through my position at the time as Research Director of the Program on Psychosocial Adaptation and the Future, Department of Psychiatry, UCLA School of Medicine, I had access to a useful body of data and research volunteers. I was in the midst of a study of television's impact on adults that involved more than 400 husbands and wives in Los Angeles.[1] They ranged in age from 20 to over 70, were generally well above the national norm in education and probably also in political awareness, and included a high proportion of conservatives, as well as liberals of all varieties. Through queries and testing our research team had collected information on their personality and demographic characteristics.

Through fresh queries to this group I obtained 207 volunteers who were assigned to the 20 IMP categories. That is, they were classified first as liberal or conservative, and then within each polarity as activists or inactivists, extremes or moderates, tough- or tender-minded, and as leaders or followers. The usual age range was separated into two groups: younger (under 45), older (over 45). This provided me with the basic IMP matrix to which the results of a special poll could be related.

Mindful of the McGregor wish-knowledge dichotomy, I designed a simple polling form to compare our respondents' personal *preferences* for president (their wishes) with their judgment about who would most *probably* be elected. My thought was that this second query, asking for their prediction of who would actually be elected, would most likely draw heavily upon their knowledge of wish-transcending social, economic, and political realities. In this way—if all went well—a productive comparison could be made between the wish-preference patterns revealed by conventional, quasi-predictive polling and the more directly predictive knowledge-probability patterns to be revealed by this second query.

Twice during the campaign my volunteers were polled.. The first mailing was early in the campaign, in February, while candidate images and the issues were still fuzzy and relatively uncrystallized. The second mailing was on June 10, with most returns in during the following week. This second mailing followed the last dramatic set of primaries on June 8, in California, New Jersey, and Ohio. By then the gales of Carterism had swept the Democratic seas of all but a few embattled hopes. The gales of Reaganism had repeatedly swamped Ford's lumbering vessel, but battered, listing, and with all aboard debating whether to abandon ship, it was still afloat.

With resources for only two polls, I thought this spacing should provide the best picture of both how and to what extent it might be possible, using this approach, to predict the future in advance.

A BRIEF DISQUISITION ON METHODOLOGY

A crucial problem in research is finding formats that clarify the data for both researcher and reader. I wrestled for some time with the data for this study and in the process uncovered a difficult but, I believe, essential principle for this kind of analysis: At this exploratory stage each type of application for IMP requires a tailoring of the method to the subject, rather than an attempt to fit everything into one or two magical, all-purpose formats.

The tables I show here are of two kinds. Tables 9.1 and 9.3 provide radically reduced matrices for ''gestalt analysis''—for focusing on relationships through being able to see the tally for the three leading candidate choices. To further aid analysis the IMP polarities are separated into the High-Forceful and Low-Forceful rankings earlier found useful in my historical study of racial attitudes. The numbers after each name are percentages for the naming of this candidate by those within each category. Thus, the first string of names, top left, for Table 9.1, shows that conservative activists were 31 percent for Reagan, 14 percent each for Ford and Rockefeller.

The second type of table further radically reduces data from these gestalt analysis tables into a simple tally for each candidate. Percentages for both High-Forceful and Low-Forceful choices for both preferred and probable selections are handled as whole numbers, independent of percentage. All categories are summed to give the five totals shown, for High- and Low-Forceful preferences and probables, and a single number total for all four.

All this, of course, represents only the surface of the complexities involved in data processing of this sort. Customarily the results appear in the terse verbal summary of the single numbers for the operationalized polls such as those of Gallup, Harris, Field, Yankelovich, or Caddell. With IMP at this stage, however, it is important to involve the reader in the kitchen, as it were; otherwise the meal will have no meaning. It may be further helpful to remind oneself we are again playing the game of futures here, our goal being to uncover rules for playing the game quite possibly similar in patternings and tallyings to those governing horse racing, GO, chess, or jai alai.

EARLY PREFERRED AND PROBABLE PRESIDENTS POLLS, FEBRUARY 1976

Among conservatives there was a remarkable uniformity in the pattern for choices of preferred president (top half, Table 9.1). Reagan was the favorite for all polarities, with Ford generally the second choice. Among liberals there was no discernible pattern, only a "mush" of sorts involving, curiously, most names for Democrats except the two who in the end ran strongest, Carter and Udall.

This picture radically changes when we examine the prediction pattern for probable president (lower half, Table 9.1). Ford springs into the lead for *all* categories for both conservatives and liberals. Reagan, however, is generally seen by conservatives as the second most probable president. Kennedy and Humphrey vie for third place. Among liber-

TABLE 9.1 IMP Sample Comparison of Preferred and Probable Presidents, February–March 1976

I. PREFERRED PRESIDENTS

High-Forceful Conservatives

A: Reagan 31, Ford 14, Rockefeller 14.
E: Reagan 43, Ford 16, Rockefeller 12.
To: Reagan 28, Ford 24, Carter 8.
L: Reagan 51, Ford 14, Kennedy 9.
O: Reagan 36, Ford 13, Rockefeller 11.

High-Forceful Liberals

A: Humphrey 13, Harris 12, Richardson 12.
E: Kennedy 17, Muskie 14, Jackson 13.
To: Richardson 13, Muskie 11, Bayh 9.
L: Humphrey 13, Richardson 12, (3 tie*)
O: Humphrey 14, Muskie 13, Kennedy 12.

Low-Forceful Conservatives

I: Reagan 42, Ford 24, Humphrey 7.
M: Reagan 27, Ford 19, Wallace 10.
Te: Reagan 40, Kennedy 13, Ford 10.
F: Reagan 22, Ford 21, Rockefeller 12.
Y: Reagan 45, Ford 20, Richardson 10.

Low-Forceful Liberals

I: Muskie 19, Kennedy 15, Jackson 10.
M: Bayh 13, Muskie 13, Humphrey 12.
Te: Jackson 18, Kennedy 15, Muskie 15.
F: Muskie 15, Kennedy 13, Jackson 11.
Y: Harris 14, Muskie 14, Bayh 13.

II. PROBABLE PRESIDENTS

High-Forceful Conservatives

- A: Ford 62, Reagan 23, Kennedy 8.
- E: Ford 68, Reagan 16, Kennedy 8.
- To: Ford 67, Kennedy 22, Reagan 6.
- L: Ford 65, Reagan 16, Kennedy 7.
- O: Ford 65, Reagan 16, Kennedy 9.

High-Forceful Liberals

- A: Ford 66, Humphrey 16, Kennedy 9.
- E: Ford 58, Humphrey 20, Reagan 8.
- To: Ford 67, Humphrey 17, Jackson 7.
- L: Ford 73, Humphrey 15, Kennedy 7.
- O: Ford 64, Humphrey 14, Reagan 10.

Low-Forceful Conservatives

- I: Ford 69, Reagan 10, Kennedy 10.
- M: Ford 63, Reagan 17, Kennedy 10.
- Te: Ford 60, Reagan 24, Humphrey 4.
- F: Ford 66, Reagan 17, Kennedy 11.
- Y: Ford 75, Kennedy 13, Humphrey 6.

Low-Forceful Liberals

- I: Ford 58, Reagan 16, Humphrey 10.
- M: Ford 66, Kennedy 13, Reagan 13.
- Te: Ford 57, Humphrey 24, Kennedy 10.
- F: Ford 55, Reagan 14, Humphrey 12.
- Y: Ford 68, Reagan 16, Humphrey 8.

*A tie between Bayh, Jackson, and Muskie, each with 10 percent.

*Code: A, activists; E, extremes; To, tough-minded; L, leaders; O, older (over 45), I, inactivists; M, moderates; Te, tender-minded; F, followers; Y, younger (under 45). Numbers following names indicate percentage of total for candidates named by respondents in category, for example 31 percent of conservative activists named Reagan as their preferred president.

TABLE 9.2   IMP Sample Presidential Prospect Scores, February–March 1976

Candidate	HiF Pref	LoF Pref	HiF Prob	LoF Prob	Total
Ford	81	94	655	637	1467
Reagan	189	176	95	127	587
Kennedy	38	56	70	67	231
Humphrey	40	19	82	64	205
Muskie	38	76	0	0	114
Jackson	13	39	7	0	59
Rockefeller	37	12	0	0	49
Richardson	37	10	0	0	47
Bayh	9	26	0	0	35
Harris	12	0	0	0	12
Wallace	0	10	0	0	10
Carter	8	0	0	0	8

als, Humphrey is second prediction for all High Forcefuls, but Low Forcefuls most often predict Reagan for this spot.

Table 9.2 provides another useful perspective. We may see here in the very high HiF and LoF Prob numbers of 655 and 637 for Ford some numerical sense of the tremendous advantage of the incumbency, which maximizes the *knowledge* factor's influence on prediction. Then in the large HiF and LoF Pref figures of 189 and 176 for Reagan we see a weighting for Reagan's preferred or wish-fueled chance to unseat the incumbent. His logical strategy is, obviously, to cut into Ford's six-to-one knowledge factor advantages by undermining confidence in Ford and projecting favorable knowledge of himself. Among liberals Humphrey's lead in preference among High Forcefuls, and weakness among Low Forcefuls, are an interesting contrast to the reverse patterns for the other leading liberals. They indicate why he was wise to stay out of the primaries: He had the established party leaders, but the followers, the vital grassroots support, simply weren't there.

Another potential for this form of analysis may be indicated by dipping into the matrix from the perspective, say, of lesser candidates and campaign managers. Rockefeller could have been heartened in his policy of "wait and see" by perceiving (Table 9.1) that even among California conservatives he was generally the third most preferred president at the time of this early poll. Richardson also could have seen good reason for remaining available. Alone among Republicans he appeared as a choice for young conservatives and activist and tough-minded *liberals*. Carter, on the other hand, could have noted that his early appeal only to tough-minded conservatives, while very interesting, indicated a long uphill struggle requiring incredible persistence and good luck.

PRIMARY AND NATIONAL ELECTION EARLY PREDICTION ANALYSIS

My main question, of course, is this: Using the IMP approach, could anything useful have been predicted for either the primaries or the national election from this early sampling?

For President Ford: With Reagan's being the preferred favorite across *all* conservative polarities, one could have predicted a serious threat in the primaries. However, since Ford was second-choice preferred president for all conservative polarities and had consensus for all polarities on first position for probable president, a prediction of containment for the threat could have been made. The outcome of the primaries certainly could not have been forecast, other than to give better odds to Ford. The fact of no support among liberals (which extended far down the line for lower rankings not shown in Table 9.1) would have given some basis for predicting Ford would have difficulty winning reelection nationally—particularly when one notes the appearance of liberals (e.g., Kennedy, Humphrey) among top conservative preferences.

For Reagan: His leading position as the preferred president for all conservative factions, and second-choice position as probable president could have supported a prediction of a serious chance to win the primary—if this was not an effect solely confined to California. Lack of liberal appeal, however, indicates no basis for predicting national election.

For Humphrey: Being first preference for three out of five High-Forceful groups, and having a High-Forceful rating of second most probable president, indicate the strength that led many professionals to predict he would be the Democratic party nominee. On the other hand, the fact that no conservatives rate him as a probable president, and moderate liberals rate Reagan as more probable, would have supported a prediction of difficulties in winning either the primary or national election.

Wallace had received much early publicity. The fact he barely showed up in this poll could have been a function of polling restricted to a small, California upper-income group. Or it could have indicated he was simply not perceived as a viable candidate by this higher educated group—a perception that soon grasped everyone.

Carter's near-invisibility at this stage, and his subsequent spectacular rise, indicate the impossibility of infallibly predicting the outcome for either the primaries or the national election at this early stage. However, we have seen how predictive information vital to candidacies, and those investing in them, could have been gathered with IMP in the early months. This estimate of usefulness seems further valid if one visualizes such a method operationalized with modern methods of polling—that is, with regular phone interviewing of a nationally distributed sample, and with fast computers data processing and reporting of results.

SECOND PREFERRED AND PROBABLE PRESIDENTS POLL, JUNE 1976

My June poll revealed both startling changes and interesting continuities. As can be seen in Table 9.3, the most dramatic change was the shift in the presidential prediction consensus from Ford in February-March to Carter in June. This consensus for Carter included all polarities except one, the older conservatives, recording a political phenomenon that experienced pundits and politicos still marvel over. Not since Wendell Willkie had anyone come out of nowhere so swiftly to seize, as Carter did in July, a presidential nomination.

This ascendency for Carter forced Ford downward in our probable presidents rating, but Ford's second-place position indicated considerable continuing strength for the incumbency. Reagan had, however, dropped to a poor third for probable president. Since this happened while he continued to gain delegates in a neck-to-neck race with Ford prior to the Republican convention, one might detect more than a little of the Goldwater phenomenon among organized Republicans. That is, out of ideological fervor Republicans had persisted in picking Goldwater to be their candidate in 1964, despite the evidence of polling and political intelligence that he couldn't possibly win election.

Among ratings for presidential preferences (top half of Table 9.3) there was relatively little change between February and June for conservatives, but for liberals much happened. The main new phenomenon was the impact of California Governor Jerry Brown. He had not been included in the list of candidates for our earlier poll. Not only had he not

announced then, but also he had specifically denied he would run-
—indeed, in a nationally televised program he had even gone on record
indicating he didn't plan to run for president, because he lacked the
necessary experience! Second only to the surprise of the Carter sweep
was the way in which Brown, though entering the campaign very late,
managed in a short time to capture a significant allegiance among conservatives, as well as liberals. Among conservatives he was third place
(after Republicans Ford and Reagan) five times and second place once.
Among liberals he ran neck and neck with Udall, who had also come
out of nowhere in my earlier poll to figure second highest to Brown
among liberal preferences. Further, regarding Brown, national polls and
his primary victories indicated that the strong showing for Brown in my
poll was not simply a function of "favorite son" loyalty for a California
sample but was a national phenomenon. Some spark in Brown fired
both liberals and conservatives nationally. It is also notable that Udall's
strength in my poll closely matched the national preference pattern
among liberals and his recurring second-place showings in national
primaries.

These trends to findings are underlined by Table 9.4, which repeats
an alternate summary format used earlier. However, now we may
clearly discern a surprise regarding Carter that Table 9.3 obscures. It is
that, while Carter leads all the rest in being predicted to win, he is
literally the *least* preferred of all candidates, liberal or conservative,
who were still being mentioned as preferences in my early June poll!

This gap has several inferential meanings. It seems to me evidence of
both the lack of familiarity with Carter as a person in June, prior to his
July nomination, and also adverse associations with his regionality-
—that is, the generally adverse image of the South held in this case by
westerners, but even more so by easterners and northerners. This complex was reflected in increasing expressions of a fear of the unknown by
Democrats before his nomination, even while national polls showed his
strength to be overwhelming. This fear was apparently suppressed by
the Democrats yearning to win the presidency during the nomination
convention, but it reemerged. The preferentiel gap for Carter also seems
a good numerical indication of the depth and breadth of the national
need for favorable information about this candidate. Before his nomination, responsive to this need, the media were already at work on the
coverage of Carterism that swelled to an avalanche prior to his election.

The nature and intensity of the media coverage following his nomina-

TABLE 9.3 IMP Sample Comparison of Preferred and Probable Presidents, June 1976

I. PREFERRED PRESIDENTS

High-Forceful Conservatives

A: Reagan 43, Ford 23, Brown 20
E: Reagan 40, Ford 31, Brown 19
To: Reagan 48, Ford 33, Rockefeller 14
L: Reagan 51, Ford 29, Brown-Rockefeller 9
O: Reagan 38, Brown 24, Ford 21

Low-Forceful Conservatives

I: Reagan 39, Ford 32, Carter-Brown 14
M: Reagan 41, Ford 24, Rockefeller 17
Te: Reagan 45, Ford 24, Brown 10
F: Reagan 34, Ford 26, Brown 23
Y: Reagan 43, Ford 33, Richardson 13

High-Forceful Liberals

A: Udall 33, Brown 23, Humphrey 20
E: Udall 32, Brown 25, Church 20
To: Brown 29, Udall 24, Church 15
L: Udall 26, Brown 20, Richardson 15
O: Brown 25, Udall 19, Church 12

Low-Forceful Liberals

I: Brown 23, Muskie 17, Carter 15
M: Brown 21, Humphrey 19, Udall 17
Te: Udall 32, Muskie 27, Humphrey 23
F: Brown 25, Udall 24, Humphrey 18
Y: Udall 34, Humphrey 25, Brown 20

II. PROBABLE PRESIDENTS

A: Carter 49, Ford 36, Reagan 15
E: Carter 51, Ford 44, Reagan 5
To: Carter 63, Ford 37,
L: Carter 37, Ford 34, Reagan 8
O: Ford 47, Carter 42, Reagan 6

Low-Forceful Conservatives

I: Carter 53, Ford 40, Reagan 15
M: Carter 50, Ford 33, Reagan 15
Te: Carter 54, Ford 42, Reagan 4
F: Carter 53, Ford 35, Reagan 10
Y: Carter 58, Ford 30, Reagan 9

High-Forceful Liberals

A: Carter 61, Ford 35, Reagan-Humphrey 2
E: Carter 57, Ford 39, Reagan-Humphrey 2
To: Carter 57, Ford 33, Reagan 7
L: Carter 60, Ford 35, Reagan 5
O: Carter 46, Ford 43, Humphrey 11

Low-Forceful Liberals

I: Carter 52, Ford 36, Reagan 12
M: Carter 58, Ford 31, Reagan 11
Te: Carter 78, Ford 22
F: Carter 55, Ford 36, Reagan 4
Y: Carter 73, Ford 25, Reagan 3

Code: A, activists; *E*, extremes; *To*, tough-minded; *L*, leaders; *O*, older (over 45). *I*, inactivists; *M*, moderates; *Te*, tender-minded; *F*, followers; *Y*, younger (under 45). Numbers following names indicate percentage of total for candidates named by respondents in category, for example, 43 percent of conservative activists named Reagan as their preferred president.

TABLE 9.4   IMP Sample Presidential Prospect Scores, June 1976

Candidate	HiF Pref	LoF Pref	HiF Prob	LoF Prob	Total
Carter	0	29	523	584	1136
Ford	137	139	383	330	989
Reagan	220	202	50	73	545
Brown	194	136	0	0	330
Udall	134	107	0	0	241
Humphrey	20	85	15	0	120
Church	47	0	0	0	47
Muskie	0	44	0	0	44
Rockefeller	23	17	0	0	40
Richardson	15	13	0	0	28

tion came as no surprise to me, for before the nominating convention I posed to myself the exercise, relevant to futures prediction, of trying to uncover the reason for Carter's sudden rise. Despite his positions on issues I noted in my last chapter, he was really not widely identified with any clearly articulated issue in the old sense. In fact, he was widely accused of "not speaking to the issues." If not issues, then where did the secret of his appeal lie? In personality? In the needs of the American people? Or in an interaction of both?

I came to the same conclusion I had earlier reached in concluding *The Healing of a Nation*: that the divisive 1960s, Vietnam, and then Watergate had created an underlying hunger in the American people for a president who radiated confidence in himself, and in themselves, and who could be trusted and believed. It was the same matrix of psychosocial needs that both Franklin Roosevelt and Adolf Hitler had sensed and responded to during the 1930s. With Carter, then, the voters had scanned the field and found among the offering this one man who best sensed this need and seemed, by the nature of the identities he projected, to fill it. I found in Carter, to my surprise at the time, a truly incredible range of "success" roles and identities to which the hopeful and the fearful might both consciously and unconsciously relate.

Catering to the American work and success ethic, he was the self-made millionaire. To conservatives, businessmen, and all those concerned about jobs and the economy, he could be perceived as the successful businessman, who "had met a payroll." To farmers—and urbanites hungering for a return to nature—he was the successful farmer. To those disturbed by divorce and the dissolution of the American family, he was the stable married man, the stable father, immersed in almost a surplus of appealing children, sisters, and relatives. To those unconsciously hungering for the archetypal matriarchal support that produced Herda in Norse and the Virgin Mary in Christian mythology there was the powerfully appealing figure of Lillian Carter, the candidate's mother. To those disturbed by the national rootlessness examined by Vance Packard in *A Nation of Strangers* there was the appeal of a man who could stand in a South Georgia field of corn immortalized on television and say, "My family has owned this ground for six generations."

To those hungering for salvation from nuclear and all other threatening forms of new technology, there was also the appeal of the man who must understand these mysteries, the college chemistry major, the graduate student in nuclear physics, the officer on a nuclear submarine. To the World War II serviceman or servicewoman—who, middle-aged, now possessed, as a generation, the greatest portion of national power—he could be perceived as one who had shared with them the experience of "the last good war." To those who, pressed by too much taxation, inflation, and unemployment, felt surely the cause was inefficiency in government, he was the successful governmental administrator, the Governor who had straightened out the mess in Georgia. To those fearful not only that America had passed its peak, but also that in fact the world might be facing annihilation without some form of superhuman intervention, there was the appeal (though few would ever admit it) of a man who had personally been "saved" or "reborn," who by his own account regularly communicated with God Himself through prayer.

Yet, curiously, for practically every one of these positive identities for some millions of Americans, there were negative counterparts for other millions. There were also many Americans who were highly suspicious of millionaires, businessmen, farmers, untainted stability, the use of mothers in politics, Southerners in any form, scientists, technocrats, military men, reformers, and, most of all, anyone sincerely religious. Moreover, as the election campaign wore on, both images seemed to waver within the consciousness of most Americans. For a time, as Carter plummeted in the polls, both the candidate and his desired constituency seemed caught within a strange web of ambivalence and uncertainty, each mirroring the state of the other. It was this double image that gave rise to the near-disastrous charges, exploited successfully by Ford and the Republicans, that Carter was "two-faced," "fuzzy on the issues," and couldn't be trusted. In the end, he was saved by the basic mathematics of party politics. There were simply more registered Democrats than Republicans, and old party loyalties——and good weather on election day—prevailed.

CONCLUSIONS

What may we conclude about methodology for futures predicting from this study? And using this methodology to test it, what did I predict?

Four conclusions seem warranted:

1. *Two-factor wish-knowledge, preference-prediction theories and heuristics are more useful than one-factor theories or heuristics.* An initiating hypothesis was that wishful thinking largely determines preferences and also voting intentions as reported to pollsters. A corollary hypothesis was that knowledge of the candidate or issue largely influences our predictions, which aren't picked up by conventional polling. If this were entirely true, the dominantly *preferred* conservative, Reagan, would have easily won a majority of the primaries and polls. Instead, the conservative race was neck and neck, the edge largely remaining with the dominantly *predicted* conservative, Ford. We could conclude that, while the tendency is for wish to determine preference and knowledge to determine prediction, both factors generally interact to determine preference, prediction, *and* reported voting intentions.

Prediction by the futurist then becomes a matter of reading the proportions of one factor to the other within the context of the ideologies and social, political, and economic facts advancing or retarding movement on an issue or candidate. In other words, however much social sciences may profitably further define these relationships, as a practical matter of contemporary futures forecasting we see wish versus knowledge, and preference versus prediction, as useful polarities to guide both questionnaire construction and data analysis. I feel they may be profitably viewed as two-factor heuristics for identifying valuable futures indicators now hidden within a collapsing of both into the single factor of voter preferences, which takes no advantage of the McGregor, Cantril, Gallup, and Delphi discoveries.

2. *My twelve-factor IMP stratification adds further to the potential*

accuracy of futures predicting. Though contemporary pollsters attempt to protect themselves by disavowing futures prediction as their primary task, their methods and results are repeatedly used to attempt this vital social task. Along with more customary demographic factors of education, income, and race, many forecasters attempt intuitively to take into account the social-psychological IMP factors I have isolated. But lacking any cohesive base in articulated theory or research, their predictions are both conceptually vitiated and lacking in confidence—and thereby in ethical marketability. My finding of IMP functional similarities across age differences and among East and West Coast samples bolsters the observation that those within any one of these strata or IMP "cells" tend more often than not to share the same beliefs with their cell mates nationally. Cantril's findings of prediction similarities among those with similar backgrounds and the degree to which our polling in this study rather closely matched national voting and polling trends again support this assumption.

Of particular significance is the fact my poll was so nonrepresentative in the conventional sense. In other words, mine was a poll of only 200 people in a single city in one region, Los Angeles in Southern California, in contrast to national samplings of 1500 people randomly selected from throughout the nation to approximate national demographic proportions. The findings of my small and other large sampling similarities has then this considerable significance theoretically and operationally. It indicates that if one's concern is futures prediction it isn't necessary to attempt conventional sampling of an entire city, state, region, or nation, which can be very expensive and hence limit applicability. It indicates that, at least for social events, futures forecasting may quite legitimately be based on the data from very small samples—if the sample is representative in depth, along the lines I have developed, rather than in breadth, along the lines of conventional polling. To combine the two methods should, of course, lead to futures predictions with a higher degree of confidence, and this could be desirable in cases of issues or candidates with a crucial bearing on our future. However, for most issues and candidates the gain in confidence for doubling-up this way could be slight in relation to the costs involved.

3. *The IMP method lends itself well to using the power of consensus versus conflict analysis.* Tables 9.1 and 9.3 make apparent the practical usefulness of separating questionnaire responses into the 10 categories for liberals and 10 for conservatives. To see those in a majority of these

categories so consistently preferring or predicting one candidate over others (for example, the Reagan over Ford et cetera preference, and the Ford over Reagan et cetera prediction) has a value for interpretation no single number, or simple rank ordering, can match. Likewise, the absence of consensus in this format, as in the case of liberal preferences in February–March, tells much at a glance. Also in regard to consensus analysis, it is notable the degree to which both liberals and conservatives were for Brown, and to lesser degrees in our poll, for Carter and Richardson. In keeping with my own projection of a new "middlistic" style for successful American and world political leadership in *The Leadership Passion*, this indicates to me the basis for predicting growing political power for these three candidates, while those associated dominantly with left or right wane.

4. *Accuracy of prediction is heavily dependent on whether there is a fixity or fluidity of social pattern and on the predictor's placement in the extension of this social patterning through time.* To all social movement there are patterns: certain small beginnings that swell developmentally into conventional or exotic shapes and then shrink in subsiding. The observation of this phenomenon extends through history from the sophistication of the compilers of the Chinese Book of Changes to Kurt Lewin in our time. In futures prediction possibly no other sensitivity is so important, for only as the predictor can sense the waxing and waning and probable patterning to social flow can he begin to predict with accuracy. For an analogy, let us use baseball and the "futuristic" challenge of throwing the ball to try to put out a runner at home plate. I speak here of throwing the baseball while stanu..g in a mudhole—or on hard ground; or in the first inning with no one on base versus in the seventh inning with bases loaded. These crucial aspects of futures prediction, to be further examined in my last chapter, are illuminated and brought easily within the grasp of the predictor by the IMP approach.

An example of the difference between predicting from fluidity versus fixity of patterning can be seen in the difference between liberal and conservative preferences and predictions in Table 9.1. The relatively stable relationships between Ford and Reagan, reflected across all IMP categories, allow one to predict a close race in the primaries. Among liberals, however, the situation reflected by Table 9.1 is so fluid, the relationships so unstable, as to make prediction highly unreliable. The most striking example of my other point, about predictor placement, is shown in the shift for probable president from Ford in February–March to the "low man on the totem pole," Carter, by June. The primaries constituted a social movement of the general type I have described: moving from small beginnings, to swell briefly into a national obsession, then to subside. Predicting the outcome for the presidency at the start of this movement, before the exposure of candidates that the primary provides, must of necessity be a high-risk, low-probability venture for the predictor. However, predicting the presidential race outcome at the close of this prefiguring social movement becomes a much lower risk venture with a much higher success probability. To collapse both points into a matter of right-brain feeling, the task of the predictor becomes to sense places of a "crystallization" within the social flow—of points in time where endings and beginnings meet in brief stabilities, and from these points then to attempt his projections.

5. *Contrary to our desire for "push button" futures prediction, by the nature of the subject and the requisite "gestalt" analysis, the capacity for prophecy must likely remain forever more art than science.* Though the thrust of my analysis is to help make intuition explicit, in numbers, orderings, and computerizing, this construction of a "prediction machine" soon reaches its limit. One problem, as Herman Kahn's ability demonstrates, is that to predict futures calls for a capacity to scan and reduce an incredible range of disparate information into single useful wholes of "gestalts." As both Messarovic and de Jouvenel stress, nothing has been found to replace man at this task. The purpose of my IMP matrix, then, is not to remove but to intensify the need for the sensitized human analyst. It can serve only to assemble information in a way aiding the predictor in his basic task of gestalt analysis. Moreover, this is only one of many sources the predictor must draw upon to read the future. One must draw upon all relevant media, studies, and polls. One must also draw upon right-brain intuition—and if necessary, the unconscious—as well as left-brain rationality. The chief advantage of IMP, and all comparable forms, is to provide analyst and seer with a gathering of data with which his imagination can roam—while at the same time constraining his imagination with boundary channels, facts, and numbers.

TEST PREDICTIONS

On the basis of IMP and the general conclusions listed above, on July 12, 1976, I formally recorded the following predictions in a letter to George Gallup, Jr., President of the Gallup Poll. Shortly before the

Democratic National Convention I predicted the obvious, that Carter would be the nominee, but also the nonobvious, that Walter Mondale would be his designee for Vice-President. A month before the Republican National Convention I predicted that Ford would be a nominee, with Reagan as running mate if "Goldwaterism" prevailed. And five months in advance of the election, I predicted that Carter would win.

I missed with Reagan, unable to anticipate Dole, and also incorrectly predicted that the race between Carter and Ford would not be close. However, this was the election year the established pollsters agreed was the most difficult ever and consistently refused to attempt any predictions. Indeed, polling's founder, Dr. George Gallup, identified the national election of 1976 as the most unpredictable since polling began. Yet with IMP's aid, I was able to predict Carter would select Mondale well before Carter himself knew he would do this, while many others were under consideration and more favored. I was also able to accurately predict that the vote for Carter would be greater than that indicated by the final polls. (This proved true for the major Gallup, Harris, and Yankelovich final polls, all of which showed less support for Carter than materialized on election day. A final Roper poll more closely approximated election results.) Most importantly, I was able to correctly predict the presidential nominees for both the Republicans and Democrats and to predict the winner of our bicentennial-year presidential sweepstakes.

Chapter 10
THE POOLING OF VISION

"The aim of every science is foresight. For the laws established by observation of phenomena are generally employed to foresee their succession. All men, however little advanced, make true predictions, which are always based on the same principle, the knowledge of the future from the past. . . . The foresight of the astronomer who predicts with complete precision the state of the solar system many years in advance is absolutely the same in kind as that of the savage who predicts the next sunrise. The only difference lies in the extent of their knowledge."[1]

This observation was made at the outset of social science by a founder who was driven by a vision we may only now, after more than 100 years, be on the verge of realizing. It was August Comte's desire to found sciences of man (psychology, sociology, political science, anthropology, history), not divorced from the physical and natural sciences, but all mutually reinforcing parts of an integrated and carefully rationalized whole. Most suggestively, he found their commonality in the shared concern of all science with the prediction of futures. As the quote also makes evident, he believed, as I do, that this capacity is in all of us, the only difference between layman and scholar being kinds and amounts of knowledge.

To this challenge to those of us who today represent his social scientific progeny, Comte added that "the determination of the future must be regarded as the direct aim of political science."[2] In view of the reduced present state of both politics and political science, it may be difficult to see why Comte should single out these activities for such a crucial social function. As I developed in terms of Washington and other American political founders in Chapter 6, and as de Jouvenel has repeatedly emphasized in his political works,[3] the reason is this: The purpose of politics is not only power but also morality—or the application of power to moral purposes. If the future is to be in any way

123

determined by man (as Comte, Marx, and Pareto hoped), desirable ends must be articulated; it is then obvious that, if the choice is either moral or immoral ends, morality will be the espoused standard, however far we are from realizing it.

This is why, in seeking principles of prediction that may generalize to all fields, I have dealt so often with political trends, currents, and behavior. My selection of material and early studies derives, not just from being fascinated by power or morality, but from the fact that, in a study of the use of the mind to predict futures, political problems, figures, and theorists provide us with the richest source of data. It was, in fact, my interest in the politically saturated Adams family, combined with some startling personal predictions, that first seriously impelled me into this investigation. Because the anecdote brings together in an experiential way many concerns elsewhere possibly overabstracted, I take time briefly to record it.

Before going to Harvard to become a historian, Henry Adams was a journalist in Washington during the Grant administration. Appalled by the corruption and degradation of ideals, he made the arresting comment that "the political dilemma was as clear in 1870 as it was likely to be in 1970." I was struck by the passage: After an early career with parallels to Adams', in 1971 I wrote and published *The Healing of a Nation*. In this book I detailed similarities of degradation during the pre-Watergate "Nixon years" to those of the Grant and Hayes presidencies of young Adams' time. Then during the early months of the Watergate revelations I found myself seized with two firm convictions, both alien to the beliefs of almost everyone I knew or read at the time.

Over a year before Richard Nixon departed I became convinced that both Spiro Agnew and Nixon would be forced from government. This conviction was so strong that, to test it, late in July of 1973 I assigned precise "cut-off" dates for the departures of both men. Nixon would be gone by one year from the time of my prediction, or by July 1974. Agnew would depart earlier, by no later than the turn of the year. This was in the days when the Watergate revelations were tumbling out, but when it still seemed highly unlikely that Nixon could be directly tied to any of it, and that he would survive. It was also before even the slightest knowledge of Agnew's malfeasance, which had *no* connection to Watergate, had surfaced. Yet I was off by less than one month in the case of Nixon: He resigned August 9, 1974. And Agnew was indeed gone before the turn of the year, suddenly resigning on October 10, 1973.

Startled when these predictions proved so accurate, I tried, informally and privately, to account for their success. (As is often the case before one become scientifically interested in a subject, these predictions were recorded with considerable precision in my own mind, but nowhere else but in the fading memories of a daughter and one or two friends.) The conclusions I reached at the time were entirely based on the use of consciousness. It seemed to me that my historical research covering 350 years for *The Healing of a Nation* had highly sensitized me to trends, cycles, and patterns governing the rise and fall of American moral purposes and expectations of and constraints upon the American presidency. Increasingly I was appalled by both the ignobility of Nixon and Agnew and by the cynicism toward and ignorance of our nation's history and purposes being expressed by most Americans. (For example, how anyone could either continue to believe in Nixon or, cynically, in his survival, after John Dean's televised testimony, was beyond me.) And I simply became convinced that acting like a magnificent leviathan beyond the comprehension of Nixon, Agnew, or the bulk of our populace, the American *system* would spew out this pair like two bad morsels, Agnew going first in keeping with the Nixon policy of offering progressively higher sacrifices in hopes of remaining in office.

This rationale seemed good at the time, but increasingly I have wondered whether something bordering on precognition might not also have been involved. It is to this question of the place and possible interplay of consciousness and unconsciousness in futures prediction I address myself in this chapter. For several reasons I have devoted most of my attention to the use of consciousness, or dominantly left-hemispheric thinking, in futures prediction. One is that we have more than 300 years of physical science and 100 years of social science that is rationality-based. This storehouse needs to be more nearly fully used for social realization, as well as for social survival. Moreover, for all the claims of the psychics, at this point in human history, left-hemispheric consciousness is the only reasonably dependable source of mind we have for dealing with the future.

On the other hand, the challenge of better prediction to guide better intervention is so severe that we would be fools indeed not to more swiftly and effectively investigate the apparently incredible predictive powers of unconsciousness, or right-hemispheric thought, to see if we may increase their dependability. It is time for social science to cease trying, on a much larger scale, to reject Freud all over again. The competition for power and knowledge underlying the psi research of the Russians, the Stanford Research Institute, Dean and Mihalasky at the Newark College of Engineering, the Maimonedes Laboratory, and UCLA, and the general climate of readiness for new paradigms among advanced thinkers in the social sciences, indicate the potential for rapid advancement in this foresaken area given either an upturn in the economy or an increase in world military and industrial threat.

In succeeding pages, I examine the implications of the pooling of consciousness, then of unconsciousness, and then of the fascinating implications of a theoretical model integrating the functions of consciousness and unconsciousness in futures prediction.

THE POOLING OF CONSCIOUSNESS

After reviewing the findings of many pages, it seems to me that a first consideration in the use of conscious mind for prediction is to define the data on which we base our predictions, or the nature of phenomena. The phenomenal world is what is presented to us daily through our senses and through memories, in contrast to the different underlying reality of electrons and atoms for physicists, or molecules and compounds for chemists. In futures forecasting, we puzzle over this sensory input trying to discern orderly trends, cycles, or patterns, and the more one looks for possible paths to the future via consciousness, the more one finds. Therefore, I attempt here to be intensive rather than comprehensive. Of many factors influencing our future this book has been concerned chiefly with the thrust of individual and group psychology, or the *ideational press*.[4] Of the number of ways by which the predictor may use such information to read the future, I briefly examine the revelations of ideational press through individuals and small groups; through its cumulation and hardening into institutions, becoming institutional press; and through cycles and patterns and dialectical flow.

Ideational Press. The purpose of my three IMP studies was to explore both the impact of ideational press on the future and to see how the future may be read through sensitivity to ideological weightings and alignments. My historical study of 200 years of American racial attitudes revealed the impact of ideational press. The Princeton study uncovered connections between leadership elite attitudes and current issues. Lastly, the West Coast study during the 1976 presidential campaign showed how wishes and knowledge may interact to shape the ideational press. All three studies further developed the case for using a limited set of ideological variables to obtain the data for a new method of processing and analyzing. This IMP method mainly consists of a matrix for visually presenting large amounts of data to the predictor in a way facilitating a wide scan and the quick detection of significant trends and patterns.

Whatever one may think of the specifics of these early studies—and I have emphasized they are intended to be exploratory and suggestive, rather than definitive—the effort seems to justify the following conclusions:

1. The influence of ideational press of both individual and group psychology on the future cannot—as some misguided theorists still persist in believing—be denied.
2. Depending on circumstances, this influence ranges from being very slight, to being (in the case of Jesus of Nazareth or Adolf Hitler) incredibly powerful.
3. This influence can be effectively measured and assigned numerical weightings.
4. Through such quantifications, it can be used to improve the prediction of futures.

I don't offer the IMP approach as a finalized and impregnably perfect entity—it is only a beginning. I do, however, feel that it represents an advancement in sophistication over most previous approaches in attempting to come to grips with ideational press, and I feel it merits further development and use by all so inclined.

Institutional Press.   With the roots of ideational press in the individual and small group defined, the matter of institutional press, which concerns sociologists, economists, and political scientists, may be easily visualized. Among the founders of our disciplines, Max Weber most effectively built this next conceptual stage. He described how the spark of ideational press in the charismatic leader catches up followers in a general conflagration of ideation, and then of how through the routinizing of charisma this ideational press becomes formalized as a church, an army, a social movement, or an industry, and thereby *institutional* press.[5]

Thus, given sufficient time, repeatedly we may see ideational press at the psychological or microcosmic level become institutional press at the sociological or macrocosmic level. Moreover, despite warnings against generalizing across disciplines, I see no reason why the matrix proposed for psychology cannot be taken over and applied to institutional press by sociologists and political scientists. I am really offering nothing more than a new way of organizing and analyzing the obvious—that policies for action are shaped by a composite of ratios within the mix of liberal to conservative, activist to inactivist, et cetera, within business, unions, the military, churches, as well as governments.

Cycles.   In considering the influence of ideational forces on the future, throughout this book I have been concerned with questions of both the nature and the direction of these forces, but of the first somewhat more than the second. In this closing chapter, I direct progressively more attention to directions of forces. A first illustration is the age-old observation of the cycling of forces: the alternation of bull and bear markets, of boom and bust, in economics; the alternation of liberal and conservative periods of national mood and political domination over our history. There are many processes involved here beyond our purview to examine (e.g., feedback systems, entropy, renewal). From the viewpoint of measurement, however—of quantifying social forces via the measurement of the beliefs of individuals—it is notable that these cycles may all be reflected in ideational shifts such as I investigated in my third IMP study of the 1976 presidential campaign. (That is, behind the amazing shift over four months to a majority belief in the election of Jimmy Carter were matters of all sorts of economics, politics, feedback, loss of hope by some candidates, and renewal of energies for others. The net result of all this activity, could, however, be measured by a few numbers and the plotting of a trend.)

Thus, from repeated assessments of group dispositions toward any question, issue, or candidate may be extrapolated the trends, the curves, and their rising, falling, or cycling, on which the majority of our predictions feed. To illustrate both the power and the pitfalls for cognition in prediction, Figure 10.1 shows examples of three kinds of trend lines. In each case the historical position of two observers (0^1 and 0^2) is noted to add a crucial element affecting prediction in each case.

In the case of the (*a*) trend we see that an observer at the earlier point in time (0^1) will tend to predict a rise or increase. The observer at the later point, however, (0^2) "foresees" a decline. In the case of the (*b*)

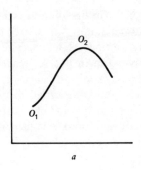

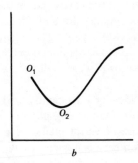

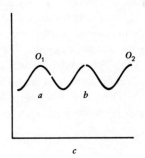

FIGURE 10.1   Trends and observers.

trend, we see the reverse: The first observer sees a decline, the second a rise. In the case of (c) trend, however, we see the "truth": that (a) and (b) trends were only portions of a longer term cycle. This is now obvious to the observer late in this sequence (0^2), who proceeds to trumpet his own "*ex post facto*" brilliance and to deride the ignorance of the audacious fools who earlier tried to predict futures. The one person safe from his contumely—and obviously our hero—is the early observer (0^1) in case (c) who foresaw neither rising nor falling by itself but the configuration of a cycle.

Patterns.   A more complex directional indicator is that of symmetric or asymmetric patterning. The configuration shown in Figure 10.2 is to suggest an ideational beginning for an issue, candidate, cause, or project at time one (T_1). It swells, picking up adherents or other measurable weightings, and also subtly shifts direction (T_2). Later still, it reaches its apogee or "golden age" (T_3), followed by denouement and end (T_4).

Though difficult to identify and quantify, and requiring the interpretative boldness necessary for forming gestalts or pattern closures, this form offers a far more powerful method for futures prediction than simple trend lines. Among phenomena I have examined, in the third IMP study it can be seen that the campaigns of all candidates except Carter and Ford operated according to configurations of this type, with both potential investors and adherents busy throughout the spring and summer of 1976 trying to sense exact shapes. More generally, this is the kind of patterning one may sense, on the microcosmic level, in the rise of any idea—for a down-to-earth example, let us say the idea of buying a new suit or dress (T_1), followed by a consideration of alternatives (T_2), an expansion of anticipations and the search (T_3), and conclusion with a purchase (T_4). This same kind of patterning operates on the macrocosmic level with the birth and death of cultures, or the beginning and end of wars.

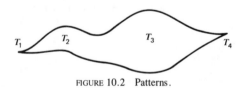

FIGURE 10.2   Patterns.

Dialectical Flow. Embracing both cycles and patterns is the dialectical flow. Metaphorically, the relation is that of the actuality of a river to its rise and fall, shaped by water supply, or to its surface configurations, shaped by terrain. The river comprises all this, but much more in terms of hydraulic dynamics. The dialectical flow is expressed in cycles and patterns, but also much more.

I have dealt elsewhere with the roots in Western philosophy, sociology, and psychology for the dialectical flow that becomes the future. Illuminated by Hegel, Marx, Pareto, Nietzsche, Weber, and Freud, sensitivity to dialectical movement is remarkably like the capacity for reading the river that Mark Twain celebrated in the river boat pilots of his masterpiece *Life on the Mississippi*. This viewpoint is being reconstructed in psychology by those resonating, for one example, to the work of Klaus Riegel, whose "Manifesto for a Dialectical Psychology" advances this orientation with compelling humor.[6] It is an elaborate orientation that, as a whole, contains much of what is presented here in parts.

The Nature of the Predictor: Cognitive Processes. The most crucial aspect of how we predict with the conscious mind are the processes we use to predict, which in turn depend on the nature of the human observer and predictor. Here it seems that much of what might be said in several volumes can, for grounding purposes, be reduced to two cognitive processes that seem to be rooted in basic motivation and learning processes, and a third important matter of cognitive stance or situation. The two cognitive processes have many names; in Chapter 4 I identified and redefined them as *scanning* and *focusing*.

We have repeatedly encountered *scanning* in this study through my identification of (1) the need to range beyond the parts to gain a sense of wholes, (2) the need for more attention to the original thoughts of Gestalt and Lewinian psychology, and (3) my articulation of this requirement with the term "gestalt analysis" in the IMP system, and the use of the IMP to improve prediction by examining a matrix of data for meaningful patterns and part–whole relationships. Scanning is also directly related to the "knowledge" component for McGregor, whose study illustrated how our predictions are composed in part of what we know, or how wide and deep our *scan* is.

We have also somewhat less often encountered *focusing*. All too briefly I noted how this other crucial component to predictive cognizing emerged in (1) the formative work of Wilhelm Wundt and William James in concepts of selective attention and apperception; (2) mention of the concepts of screening, filtering, and categorizing in my summary of Ornstein's book; and (3) the demonstrational focusing of the IMP system. The three studies scanned 200 years of American history, hundreds of opinions of Princeton students, and preferences and predictions for all major candidates for the 1976 presidency, to repeatedly *focus* on a few salient elements. This crucial component of prediction was noted as a dominant characteristic of John Quincy Adams' "peculiar mind." According to Brooks Adams, it "concentrated slowly but when centered it acted with extreme intensity."[7] Focusing is also related to the "wish" component of McGregor, in the sense that motivation guides our focusing on particular subsets of data for abstraction. Focusing is also guided by the "ego-involvement" that McGregor felt was more important than breadth of knowledge in accounting for accuracy of prediction. (Again, may I note my Chapter 4 clarification—that what McGregor had in mind seems, in the terms of modern creativity research, to be "task-involvement" rather than "ego-involvement.")

Categories of these types I characterize as scanning and focusing are often only *ad hoc* selections by the writer for the convenience of the reader. It is important to realize that this is not solely the case here, but that in fact much evidence exists to indicate these are closely interacting, functionally interrelated processes fundamental to all learning. In other words, we automatically use both processes to gather and evaluate all the sensory information we are continually receiving; the results of our analysis then guide our actions daily. Futures prediction then becomes but a more highly organized and cognizant use of this everyday capacity. We marshal our minds and aids (books, observations, matrices, computers) to, first, take in all possible relevant information bearing on the future, and second, to discard all but a radically limited subset of this information for concentrated analysis.

The Nature of the Predictor: Cognitive Situation. Another basic matter regarding conscious "futurizing" is that of the cognitive stance or situation, or *placement of the observer*. I have already noted both the pitfalls and potential power of the perspective of the observer, which Einstein used to establish the theory of relativity, in predicting trends. This observer placement is even more critical in pattern reading. From the time of the Chinese who compiled *I Ching* to the perceptions of

Comte and Henry Adams, it has been observed that potentially meaningful patterns flow in sequences of potentially meaningful phases.
Cognitive reading of the future then becomes a matter of correctly
identifying *both* pattern and phase.

In Figure 10.3, for example, an observer in phase one (P^1) might
have difficulty identifying either the pattern or the phase for the movement (ideational, social, whatever) of his interest. Possibly by the time
he has personally reached phase two (P^2) within this movement, however, he is able (from past experience) to recognize that he is probably
involved in a pattern of type X rather than type Y. From this sense of
placement in phase two (and generally that is all it can be, a *sensing*
rather than firm knowledge), he is then able to project the nature of
phases three and four yet to come. He is now in a position to not so
mysteriously—entirely with conscious cognizing—predict the future
with some degree of accuracy.

A good example of this type of conscious pattern reading is one
"knowable root" to John Quincy Adams' seeming uncanny power to
predict the Civil War. It is evident from Brooks Adams' account that his
grandfather, John Quincy, definitely connected the invention of the
cotton gin by Eli Whitney in 1793 with the Civil War, which began in
1861, by sensing the following sequence of phases.[8] Unknown generally today, but a vivid piece of knowledge for the moral mind of
Adams, was that slavery had been dying of "natural causes" prior to
Whitney's invention. But suddenly there appeared this new technology,
potentially revolutionary in impact because of its capacity to speedily
remove the tenacious seeds from the wanted cotton strands. Whitney's
invention meant that cotton, hitherto a minor crop, could now become
big business—but only if there was sufficient slaves to work the fields
and to gather up the mountains of cotton bolls required to feed this
ravenous and monstrously efficient new device. And so Adams could
foresee the future through his understanding of how this invention related to the most significant pattern to American social movement in the

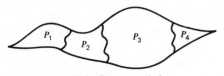

FIGURE 10.3   Patterns and phases.

1800s: The cotton gin (phase one) brought on the fresh need for slaves (phase two), which inevitably increased the tension between North and South (phase three), leading to the Civil War (phase four).

This example is of particular interest because it is an instance from the last century of one of the most highly developed types of forecasting today: the projection of outcomes in terms of *systems* impact from the development of new technology.[9] The pattern analysis I applied to the cotton gin applies to the invention of the automobile, the airplane, the computer, television, and will no doubt increasingly apply to the more recent invention of the laser and holography.

The Nature of the Predictor: Personality Processes.   So far, in cognition and situation, I have considered general processes. The thrust of my studies of ideology and the development of IMP is that the predictor is also heavily influenced by personal differences. In physics this is the observer problem central to relativity theory, articulated by Einstein and Heisenberg.[10] In social science, it is the problem of group differences explored by sociology and individual differences explored by psychology.

In practical terms, it means this for futures predicting. If we are to increase the accuracy of predictions, we must uncover and carefully take into consideration the personal and social biases of the predictor. This is true whether we are protecting ourselves against the distortion of our own differences or the differences of others. One implication of my IMP studies is that all serious Delphi studies should test, define, and attempt to balance their participations in terms of the IMP categories. Another implication is that those who use the services, or attempt evaluations of the work, of futurists, should be sensitive to their likely personal biases.

For example, in left versus right terms, Herman Kahn and Daniel Bell are dominantly norm-maintainers, whereas Willis Harman and Robert Theobald are dominantly norm-changers. Inevitably, these differences will color their views. Kahn and Bell, for example, tend to see the future as a relatively choiceless extension of one of the worst norm-maintaining features in our present society—namely, the centralization of control pointing toward the giant empire of a bureaucratic equilibrium, or what Kahn calls the "Augustinian Age."[11] By contrast, Harman and Theobold see the future as being one of swiftly dwindling choices between two main alternative futures. One is life under the bureaucratic bludgeon. The other is a truly humanistic society that can only come to be through a fundamental departure from the past- —through what Harman calls "a transformation of truly awesome magnitude."[12]

Conventional wisdom would hold that one should avoid all those with explicit or implicit ideologies and seek ideal "neutralists." Such moves can, however, lead one to the worst of all ideological traps, that of the avowed predictor who hedges his bets in obfuscation and self-protective mediocrity. To have any kind of useful insight into the future one must be animated to *care* about the future; and intelligence—as the works of Kahn and Bell, as well as of Harman and Theobald amply illustrate- —*can* transcend ideology.

The Pooling of Conscious Mind.   In addition to the operation of the individual conscious mind in predicting futures, this book has marshaled evidence for the pooling of individual predictions to achieve group predictions. This evidence includes the McGregor, Cantril, and the Kaplan, Skogstad, and Girshick studies, the Gallup Poll findings, and the general thrust to the best of the Helmer, Dalkey, Gordon, and other Delphi studies. These works seem to provide a compelling case for the following propositions:

1. By "pooling" the capacity of individuals it is possible to attain an appreciable increase in the accuracy of predictions.
2. One part of this increase in accuracy comes from the radical multiplying of scanning capacities made possible by drawing on the knowledge and experience of many, rather than of a single mind.
3. Another part of this increase in accuracy comes from the structuring and intensifying, or focusing, that group prediction methodologies bring about. The structuring comes from having highly specific and well-constructed questions presented in the orderly fashion made possible by questionnaires. The intensifying comes both from competency and achievement drives, or the desire to perform at one's highest level, and from group conformity pressures, or the need to apply one's mind successfully as others are trying to do.
4. Another part of this increase in accuracy comes from the central point stressed by Helmer and all perceptive users of Delphi and its variants, and made explicity by the Kaplan, Skogstad, and Gershick study: that the initial prediction should be reached by the individual

isolated from the distorting influences of the customary group dis-
cussional situation. (This does not, however, rule out the possibility
of better prediction through open discussion within the ideally, ergo
very rare, symbiotic group.)

5. Another part of this increase comes from the aspect of Delphi
methods calling for intensive continuing research—the nature of the
individual predictor. Expertise and nonexpertise have both been
shown to add to, as well as detract from, group predictive accuracy;
expertise plus psi abilities appears promising—the matter should be
clarified.

6. A final main portion of the increase in accuracy then comes from the
power of data processing and statistical analysis. By processing individual opinions (or "portional" visions) to obtain both the measure
of central tendency (the average,, majority vote, median), and by
juxtaposing this information with the measure of variation (the
range, the spread from "high" to "low"), both scanning and focusing are graphically maximized. To guide his predictions, the predictor now has in hand a highly abstracted and structured quantification
of "group predictive mind."

If one examines the evidence and analyzes the process in this manner,
it seems obvious to us that the final product of "group mind" or "pooling" will *generally* be superior to predictions by the individual, no
matter how gifted. This is not to pose infallibility for such methods, nor
to say they don't need further improvement, nor to suggest that the
gifted individual may never outperform the group, nor to intimate that
there are not many potential pitfalls in "pooling" methods. I simply
emphasize that, if we consider, on one hand, the technical and logical
difficulties of futures prediction, and on the other, the social necessity
for attempting to do so, the pooling of consciousness offers us a tool we
must speedily now investigate and use more effectively.

THE POOLING OF UNCONSCIOUSNESS

I characterized the use of consciousness to predict futures as a matter
of reading phenomena. To one of the key philosophers in the shaping of
modern mind, Immanuel Kant, phenomena were the surface to reality,
which we apprehend and deal with through our eyes, ears, nose, and the
rest of our sensory equipment as humans. In contrast was the much
vaster reality beyond our radically limited sensing—a world that we

could only intuit, and then try, through theorizing and the testing of theories, to make cognitive sense of through our intuitions. This larger reality—to which we seem to be linked by our unconscious mind in ways difficult to define—Kant characterized as the *noumena*.[13]

It was this "other reality" that Brooks and Henry Adams were, toward the ends of their lives, trying so frenziedly to apprehend by the seemingly strange alchemy of mixing physics with history. While Henry grappled with noumenal concepts of forces and vectors, Brooks noted: "My inference was this in 1893: Mostly men work unconsciously, and perform an act before they can explain why; often centuries before."[14]

The evidence for precognition that we examined in Chapter 5 presents a picture of many observations of phenomena, a small opening wedge of fascinating experiments to define it, and some scraps of amorphous and unorganized theory. To gain some better means of purchase on this strange stuff, let us compare what we know of the operation of the use of conscious mind in prediction with what seems to operate with unconscious mind. One important difference is that here we do not find the same kind of observationally supported links between past, present, and future we sketched for consciousness. We may through dream analysis and Jungian and Freudian therapies feel we discern something comparable to the trends, cycles, and patterns of external reality. However, there must then come to anyone who seriously investigates precognition an inescapable sense of a *direct jump*.[15] From what we know of the operation of conscious mind, we may speculate there are intervening processes comparable to trend, cycle, or pattern interpretation. And experimental methods as yet unknown may tease out supportive evidence for such a view. It remains our conviction, however, that something else, or something additional, is involved. There is this sense of a leap that operates according to principles different from those with which we have become familiar in our relatively few centuries of developing rationality. It also has the feel of a leap in taking us across such a conceptual gulf into another, or separate, reality.[16]

It has become fashionable, of course, among those who prefer to think of consciousness as somehow miserably deficient and "old hat" to think of this other reality as truly separate—that is, as operating in no way at all as we do in consciousness. This seems to me an unprofitable case of "reverse discrimination" on the part of those whose interests have been so long, and so unfairly, excluded by modern science. For surely, if sentient mankind has learned anything over the centuries, it is this dictum from Plato through Spinoza to Einstein: Whatever this is that we experience and are part of, it is bound together by some body of common law.

For example, it again seems apparent that the two central principles I identified in conscious prediction, scanning and focusing, do also operate in prediction through unconsciousness. The connection is apparent in the observation I quoted earlier of the characteristics of John Quincy Adams' mind. His mind "concentrated slowly"—during which time we may assume he was scanning to assimilate vast quantities of information. This was followed by the centering, in which his mind "acted with extreme intensity." And then occurs this highly suggestive passage in Brooks' account, linking conscious to unconscious mind: *"Once absorbed he lapsed into a species of trance in which he forgot all else."*)[17]

In modern experimental work with precognition there are at least two instances I know of that demonstrate both principles at work. One is the Brier–Tyminski study described in Chapter 5. The other is the procedure developed by Dr. Barry Taff at UCLA for developing telepathy in nonpsychics through conditioning, or more specifically, positive feedback and reinforcement. This procedure involves relaxing a group in a dark room free of noise or any other distraction. Participants are then asked to clear their minds of all clutter and to free associate (scanning) and report all images that might be associated with (focusing) a specific stimulus word.[18] This procedure has been used to explore precognition informally; as I finish this book, pilot testing for formal experiments is underway.

Earlier, for the use of consciousness in prediction, I noted the importance of the nature and situation of the observer. Here there is much evidence of a similarity between the operation of conscious and unconscious mind. Dr. Thelma Moss, by training and in practice a clinical psychologist, has compiled extensive observations of how psi experiences are shaped by both the observer's personality and occupational situation.[19] Over several years of developmental telepathy work involving hundreds of participants of both sexes, Dr. Taff has observed that, contrary to stereotype, the capacity for psychic voluntary performance seems to be more prevalent in men than in women.[20] Sex differences, as well as personality differences in psi abilities, have been extensively documented by Dean and Mihalasky.[21] While too complex for quick summarizing these findings emphasize that the nature and placement of the observer are as crucial in reception of meaning through unconscious as through conscious mind.

Particularly noteworthy in the case of the relation of observer to prediction by unconscious mind are two prevailing kinds of precognitions. One is the "warning" type I earlier characterized as arousing "survival" motivation, as in the case of Lincoln's preassassination dream. In the other type, which occurs in dreaming or waking trances, one senses a kind of accidental "straying" by the mind into this separate or other reality, while the defenses of consciousness are weakened or let down.

However it may come to be, there remains this feeling of a leap or jump from the world we know with our senses, into a different world we intuit. After 300 years of physics and chemistry, of the fact that a radically different world is "out there" there can be no doubt. But of what surmises tell us of its prime characteristics we cannot help but doubt, and resist implications, and insist there must be another explanation. For we are told the two prime characteristics of this other reality are that it has neither time nor space as we know them. "When we get down to the atomic level, the objective world in space and time no longer exists," the great physicist Werner Heisenberg wrote in his autobiography.[23] In place of the time we divide into past, present, and future, there is a simultaneousness of all events. In place of space, which we know as three-dimensional (height, width, and depth), or (by adding time) as four-dimensional, there is only a possibly endless multidimensionality.[24]

The difficulty is, even if this is the case, how may we visualize it? For visualization is the *sine qua non* for life in this phenomenal world, and without some means of visualization we cannot hope to surmount such a conceptual hurdle. As a heuristic beginning, I offer Figure 10.4, in essence an abstraction of no more than what we observe happening in this reality when we drop a stone into a pond. The stone dropping into the water creates a multidirectional tension, which moves out from the central point in widening concentric rings or force fields. In our consideration, the equivalent for the stone is the memorable event, which Freud, the Gestaltists, and Lewin all explored in terms of the event's capacity for inducing *tensions* that seek expression or relief. Could this tension adhering to events be the link between phenomena and noumena, as well as between consciousness and unconsciousness?

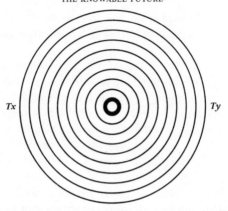

FIGURE 10.4   Perception of events in multidimensionality.

Most suggestively, this image of the stone dropped into the pond came to me in advance of reading of Putthof and Targ's "advanced potential" theory (Chapter 5), which makes use of the same image to convey a possibility of relationships that had independently occurred to me. That is, if the tensional event occurs in hypothetical "timelessness," to a psychic perceiver living in the present Time X (Tx in Figure 10.4) it will be apprehended precognitively, as radiating from the future. To a psychic observer living in Time Y (Ty in Figure 10.4) it will be apprehended retrocognitively, or as radiating from the past.

I return briefly to this prospect in considering the relation of conscious to unconscious mind in later pages. To conclude this consideration of the possibilities of prediction through unconscious mind, I must ask what evidence there is that anything comparable to the potential for the "pooling of vision" with conscious mind also exists with unconscious mind? The only answer I can give at this point is that there is, as yet, no "hard" evidence for such a possibility. But for a variety of reasons—East–West competition, exhaustion of the paradigms of social science, the concern of physical scientists for solving the problems of both predicting and shaping the future—I would myself predict it will not be long before such "hard" evidence emerges.

RIGHT, LEFT, AND FOREBRAIN

In keeping with an explosion of popular and scientific interest in brain functions, to this point I have centered my observations on futures predicting on our neglected right- versus our dominant but limited left-brain capacities. Now let us all too briefly examine how information from both halves seems to be consolidated or "pooled" in terms of brain function.

From sources even more neglected than those dealing with right-brain functions, neuropsychologist and futurist David Goodman has pulled together the case for the primacy of the *forebrain* in futures forecasting.[25] Here the evidence derives largely from examining behavior change in victims of the once highly popular prefrontal lobotomies. This grim operation is of retrospective interest because it literally cut off much of the right- and left-brain half capacities from the the frontal lobes, or forebrain. At first prefrontal lobotomies were hailed as a great success in relieving anxieties and making the lobotomized more outgoing and likable, with no apparent loss in intelligence. But then observers began to note other significant changes. Underneath an amiable facade, the lobotomized were abnormally self-centered, were unable to relate to others emotionally, had blunted ethical and moral sensitivities, and had lost a "social sense." "The adult virtues- —altruism, self-sacrifice, patriotism—that required an appreciation of a whole greater than the self disappeared, as if erased."[26]

Here then is the basis in brain functioning for our rationale in Chapter 6 for the apparent connection between a sense of moral responsibility for one's group and a capacity for futures forecasting. John Woolman, George Washington, John Quincy Adams, and Abraham Lincoln were my cases in point. All four of these great Americans, three of them political leaders, were notably moral men. They all also had so highly developed a social sense as to make them almost alien beings in comparison with the run-of-the-mill human. To these forebrain-locational capacities was added the uncanny ability of all four to foresee the future. Could morality and social sense then be linked to the capacity for future prediction via forebrain functions? Where there clues in the behavior of the lobotomized? Just as one might expect, the great remaining lack in the lobotomized was that they were unable to plan for, visualize, or anticipate the future in any meaningful way.

Soviet neuropsychologist A. R. Luria has characterized our forebrain functions as being threefold: foresight—including the detection of patterns of change; systems thinking—or the ability to cognize in wholes; and self-regulation—or the ability to control the behavior that comprises one's own future by interposing something that *governs*, that says yes I will do this or no I will not do that, between stimulus and response.[27] To these forebrain powers Goodman suggests there should be added

"holos," or the social sense, and "prognos," or the future sense-
—including goal-directed *selective attending*.

It seems evident, then, that our capacity for foreknowledge derives
from pooling and processing by the forebrain of rational left-brain information and intuitive right-brain information. In other words, it is as
though the forebrain acts like a field general to whom two lieutenants
bring in reports from the heat of battle. One lieutenant, representing left
brain rationality, is spotlessly uniformed, clicks his heels and rattles off
his information like a computer. The other, representing right brain
intuition, silently slips in clad in his spy's gypsy disguise and mumbles
and rambles through his account. The forebrain as field general then
sifts the perceptions of both lieutenants and decides what is the likely
shape of the future course of battle, and what is to be done about it.

WHOLE MIND AND REALITY

To this point I have constructed a tripartite view of how mind seems
to operate in predicting futures. Under forebrain monitoring and guidance, we find conscious mind processing the information from the
phenomenal world much as a computer with pattern recognition equipment would.[28] It scans the data; if it then detects anything coinciding
with the trends, cycles, and patterns with which it is programmed, it
will predict future events. Also with forebrain monitoring, we find
unconscious mind processing information apparently from the
noumenal as well as phenomenal worlds—but unlike a computer it
seems to apprehend the future directly. Rather than there being solely a
reference to the time-based experience represented by a computer's
programming, it seems to directly tap into another omnipresent source
of information—or it seems to actually *see* rather than project or *fore*see
events. How can we reconcile two such seemingly disparate operations,
particularly when one of our necessary bodies of data is so unacceptable
to most social scientists?

One way to begin to achieve such a reconciliation is to request of
social scientists the open-mindedness that, as Koestler documents, increasing numbers of physical and natural scientists are able to bring to
this type of surmising.[29] Why should this be? One reason is that physical and natural science has had longer for the exhaustion and renewal of
paradigms. Another reason is that social scientists must, by the nature
of their discipline, be almost exclusively concerned with phenomena.

By contrast, to gain any advancement whatsoever, long ago the physical scientist was forced to seek beneath the phenomenal suface for the atomistic other reality of the noumena. And so I ask my fellow social scientists: How satisfied are you with our present paradigms? Do you feel at times a sense of suffocation? Do you feel they may, for the time being, be exhausted? Why not then at least take a look at a possible source of renewal?

Two ways suggest themselves to me as avenues toward reconciling the differences of conscious and unconscious mind, and of the phenomenal and noumenal worlds. One way is to explore the implications of *tension* as a bridging concept between the two kinds of worlds. Earlier I advanced the analogy of a memorable event's acting like a stone thrown into a pond, which creates tension within the surrounding medium. In the pond there is a pressure upon molecules, forcing the widening rings. In conscious mind, as the Gestaltists and Lewin showed, there is a comparable tensional pressure forcing disequilibrium and creating the need for regaining equilibrium.[30] In unconscious mind, there are the cathexes of Freud, the thrusts toward wishfulfillment.[31] In social change, as Weber demonstrated with the conceptual flow of charisma to routinization, the same pattern may be discerned over and over again.[32] In physics, for an extreme example, there is the atomic explosion.

Such tensional thrusts in the phenomenal world must have equivalents in the noumenal world. May we not then surmise the human observer who, for some reason, receives vibrations from the noumenal event before it becomes phenomenal? May we not surmise that, as shown in Figure 10.5, by radiating outward in a configuration approximating what we know as "beginning, middle, and end," these vibrations might be received as a gestalt by the psychic observer? And is it then so inconceivable that this same gestalt might be applied by the psychic observer to detect a correspondence of patterns in this phenomenal world we inhabit? Or that from a position in time early in the pattern he then predicts what is to come?

It does seem logical that something of this sort may operate, but such an explanation could account only for the pattern, not the details, and one of the most startling characteristics of many apparent precognitions is the wealth of detail. Another explanation is called for; the most compelling we have found combines Plato's "Allegory of the Cave" with the modern discovery of holography.

Kant's concept of the phenomenal versus the noumenal worlds had its

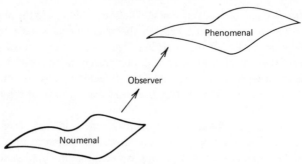

FIGURE 10.5   Dual-reality events and the observer.

roots in Plato's *Republic* and the searching analysis of human cognition advanced by Plato with his famous "allegory of the cave."[33] He likened the cognitive situation of mankind to that of slaves chained in a deep cave with their backs to the entrance. This entrance to the cave receives the full force of the sunlight. Just within the entrance a puppet show using fully dimensional forms is being conducted by puppetmasters to enact the drama of real life. But all the slaves can see are the silhouettes of the puppets, which, projected by the fierce sunlight, dance on the back of the cave.

As Plato saw it, this dance of flat images, conveying only the distorted shadows of the "true" reality, is what we "chained slaves" perceive, and attempt to understand, and must by our sensory limitations classify as reality. (And if a slave should escape his chains, and for the first time see the sunlight and return to try to tell his fellow slaves about it, Plato predicts they would, in fear and disbelief, kill him. Therein lies the eternal tale of popular receptivity to mind's advance.) Later in history, within the formative years of Christianity, Paul again expressed this view of our world as only a projected image in his first letter to the Corinthians. This is the philosophical root to his arresting "Now we see as in a glass darkly, but then face to face."[34]

Nearly 2000 years pass, and then in 1947, while searching for a way to improve the electron microsocpe, British physicist and futurist Dennis Gabor conceived of the principles of holography, an achievement for which he received the Nobel Prize. Then in 1960, by using the then new discovery of laser beams as a light source, Dr. Howard Maiman of Hughes Aircraft Company created the first working holographic image. By now most of us are aware of this amazing phenomenon—how we may see a projected three-dimensional image of an object so "real" that, as we move, its aspect changes just as though it were the object itself. Technically, this is achieved by splitting a single beam of laser light, one half hitting the object directly, the other half reflected to hit the object at an angle. These two different images are projected upon a film, which may be either photographic or the film formed by the surface to water (or any other fluid). Within the film these images reside in an interference pattern that reveals, as if by magic, a fully dimensional image of the object being holographed.[35]

Two features of holography are of great interest here. One is that we may see, expressed through a startling modern technology, an amazing replication of Plato's vision of the cave. We see again an object that appears to us to be remarkably real but that in fact is nothing more than the substanceless projection of a real object that may be hidden from us in such demonstrations. We see in modern "hardware" an analogue for the phenomenal world as image and the noumenal world as reality.

The other feature of interest is that, unlike any other medium previously discovered, the hologram contains all the information it receives in each of its particles. If you were to slice an ordinary photographic negative in half, you would, of course, be left with only half the image originally recorded. With a hologram, however, you may slice it into ever smaller particles, and although progressively fuzzier, each particle will contain the whole image. To account, then, for the operation of precognition, Dr. Barry Taff has theorized that not only the brain and mind but also its larger 'home,' the noumenal universe, operate like a hologram in two ways. One: Our phenomenal world is a projection upon the "film" of three-dimensional matter from the "other reality." And two: We occasionally foresee the future by tapping into one "particle" of the noumenal world, which acts like a hologram to hold all information simultaneously.[36]

How could past, present, and future all be stored simultaneously in any one medium, no matter how vast? It has been estimated that within a man-made hologram the size of a single book page the entire *Encyclopedia Brittanica* can be stored.

But what about free will? What about our crucial ability to intervene to change as well as predict futures? For it would seem that such a view mandates a completely deterministic viewpoint. This is true if we visualize the noumena as a single giant hologram. However, at all levels in this phenomenal world, from the activity of amoebas in pond water to the clustering of galaxies in the skies, we may observe the phenomena of large units "afloat" in a medium, and these units may or may not interconnect. It seems reasonable, then, to postulate that, if the noumena operate at all according to holographic principles, they could be visualized as a flotation of holograms, within each of which activity would be determined, but offering freedom in "choice" of "hologram." Precognition would then be "intra-hologram," but to cross the space between "holograms" would be another matter altogether, beyond visualization.

It is a shame Henry Adams had to die before this age that may have found the technology to articulate the theory toward which he so magnificently floundered in trying to reconcile phenomena and noumena.

"Always and everywhere the mind creates its own universe, and pursues its own phantoms," Adams wrote in the final pages of his essay on phases. "But the force behind the image is always a reality—the attractions of occult powers. If values can be given to these attractions, a physical theory of history is a mere matter of physical formula, no more complicated than the formulas of Willard Gibbs or Clerk Maxwell, but the task of framing the formula and assigning the values belongs to the physicist, not to the historian; and if one such arrangement fails to accord with the facts, it is for him to try another, to assign new values to his variables and to verify the results. The variables themselves can hardly suffer much damage."[37]

Causal, Teleological, and Synchronistic Mind. This exploration has taken us to such outer (some would say "far out") reaches of the mind, it is desirable to now return to earth, so to speak, and summarize the operation of conscious and unconscious mind as it relates to futures prediction.

We are most familiar, then, with the use of forebrain and left-brain consciousness to project futures in terms of causal relationships, such as $A \rightarrow B$, or $A + B = C$. This is the underlying paradigm for my IMP system and all similar methods of futures prediction.

I have also posed the nature of another, more advanced operation of consciousness, still causal, that predicts futures through the recognition of established *patterns* to growth. Ira Progoff has characterized this view as "teleological": We perceive that phase A possibly leads to phase B, to phase C, to phase D, and so on.[38]

By examining both the known mechanisms of consciousness and the possible mechanisms of unconsciousness, however, we have vaulted in this final chapter toward a theoretical view wedding the two realms. This wedding may be visualized as shown in Figure 10.6. Here *A* represents the phenomenal (or physical, sensate, perceived) world with which we are most familiar. It is characterized by three dimensions, height, breadth, and depth, and by a fourth dimension added by the movement and duration of three-dimensional objects through time. In terms of the hologram analogy, this is the realm of the image.

This world familiar to us as sensate humans then, in a sense, "floats within" (or is parallel to, coexists with, or is synchronistic to) the other reality shown in Figure 10.6 as the *B* surround. This is the noumenal (spiritual, "pure" energy, nonmaterial) world that we apprehend by intuition, by abstractions such as this, and possibly directly through some forms of precognition. It is characterized by being both a spaceless and timeless multidimensionality, and by causality in forms other than those with which we are acquainted. In terms of the hologram analogy, this is the realm of objective reality.

The Pooling of Mind. Possibly with the ambiguous comfort of these explanations I have advanced for an otherwise mystifying whole, it may now be possible to more swiftly put to use the human capacity I have characterized as the pooling vision. Certainly by now there should

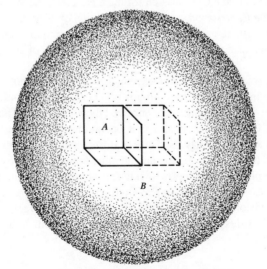

FIGURE 10.6   A noumenal–phenomenal whole.

remain nothing very mysterious or offputting about this form of human technology. "Considering that even now we are unable to foretell the weather by means of its determining factors, it is not surprising that mankind should remain attached to presages and omens," de Jouvenel writes of the earliest known forms of the pooling of vision. "The scientists confess that a study of air movements does not enable them to predict a period of abnormal cold more than a month in advance. But in the autumn of 1962 everybody in my countryside foretold a hard winter, pointing to such signs as the abundance and brightness of red berries on rockspray and firethorn. They were using the oldest of all methods of prediction: the reading of presages or omens."[39]

So here we see a kind of pooling of observation that has operated since the earliest sentient life on earth. An event occurs. It is associated with something else. Over centuries this association is repeatedly noted until it passes into folk wisdom. This folk wisdom may then either be classified as superstition by science, or, as in the case of penicillin, be used by science to guide the formally useful "discovery."

Taking the broad view, I also think that this pooling of vision I have identified in the context of both conscious and unconscious mind operates today wherever two or more minds gather to consider the prospect for prophecy or futures forecasting. Luncheons, seminars, symposia; the present handful of institutes, centers, departments, and programs for futures research; the Commission for the Year 2000; the World Futures Society; *The Futurist* magazine; the publication of every article or book to this end—all are examples of a pooling of vision to the same purpose de Jouvenel originally visualized with his concept of a "surmising forum."

While I was finishing this book, he cautioned: "I do not share your confidence in forecasting by a group. I do believe in the confronting of surmises by individuals having conceived them in silence. There are, as my friend Olaf Helmer said, secret operations of the mind whereby something appears clearly. Because of different combinations of stored knowledge (of the past, there being no other knowledge in my vocabulary), something which appears to you but not to me, and something else which appears to me and not to you, gives rise to a vision. Such individual visions can then be confronted and puzzled over together in a construction-destruction process. But they must be formed individually."[40]

Of his own hopes for the surmising forum, he earlier wrote the words that first best crystallized for me this theme I have emphasized.

"We are forever making forecasts—with scanty data, no awareness of method, no criticism, and no cooperation. It is urgent that we make this natural and individual activity into a cooperative and organic endeavor, subject to greater exigencies of intellectual rigor. Who will fulfill this social function? It is naturally incumbent on those whose object of study is society, or better still man in society."[41]

Chapter 11
THE CHOSEN FUTURE

From the visions of George Washington and John Quincy Adams to the bicentennial-year election of Jimmy Carter and Walter Mondale, we have examined the sensing and choosing of political, social, and economic futures. From the challenge of August Comte to the contemporary response of Kahn, Helmer, de Jouvenel, the Club of Rome scientists, McClelland, McGregor, Cantril, Gallup, and the precognition explorers, I have probed for substance and structure for an adequate new psychology of prophecy. And now I must rather cold-bloodedly ask, does all this research and thought really matter? Or is this book just another heady intellectual entertainment for the declining years of the Great American Dream?

Earlier I noted that our relation to the future is dialectical and two-sided. It involves not only prediction, which this book concentrates on, but also intervention. In this other half to the futures relationship, we use predictions of doom to "beat" them, to prove them wrong, or as a spur to shape the future to humanistic ends. The difference is that between the seer, who perceives both bad and good prospects, and the visionary—of whom Buckminster Fuller[1] is prototypical—who states the ideal or utopian goal.

The success of prediction or intervention can be proved only by the future. *We do know, however, that in small but vital ways the future is chosen.* To clearly pose this matter of choice, I use the contemporary issues identified in Chapter 8—as well as one other that has become personally meaningful, namely sexual equality—to project two scenarios. One is of the chosen future for "the foreknowing society," in which the concerns I seek to express are strenuously pursued. The other is of the chosen future for "the drifting society," in which the futurist tasks are either ignored or treated as harmless entertainments for an ineffectual coterie. These two futures are seen from the perspective in the year 2000 of myself as, in the first case, a reasonably optimistic, and in the second, a deeply pessimistic, 75-year-old man.

THE FOREKNOWING SOCIETY

Following its foreshadowing during the presidencies of John Quincy Adams, Theodore and Franklin Roosevelt, John Kennedy, and Lyndon Johnson, the foreknowing society gradually became an effective reality during the Carter, Mondale years. The most evident moves through government were administrational. An interdisciplinary group of forecasters comparable to the Council of Economic Advisors was created (reporting directly to the President, this was the group jocularly known as "The White House Prophets"). The forecasting function of the Office of Budget and Management (OBM) was expanded; important forecasting advisory groups were created by Congress; both governmental and private forecasting (e.g., Stanford Research Institute, Brookings, Hudson, Rand, etc.) were coordinated by a special office of the OBM. Less evident, but of appreciable impact, were certain presidential and vice-presidential emphases deriving from personal backgrounds. In retrospect it seems evident that Carter's support for forecasting was linked to the tradition and function of prophecy in the Bible, as well as to his unusual grounding in systems analysis and operations research. For Mondale comparable influences may be discerned in the religious steeping of this son of a Lutheran minister and in the underlying Scandinavian "planned society" ethos of his native Minnesota.

As many feared—and the famous Executive Strike of 1980 dramatized—if government had acted alone, the result could have been disastrous. However, after a close call in, prophetically, 1984, the danger of overwhelming governmental forecasting power was contained by the rising strength of the "anti-Big Brother forecasting baronies." One such "barony" was formed by the increase in sophisticated and socially oriented forecasting by business. Another was composed of independent new forecasting services akin and often allied to the earlier opinion polls. The third offsetting power came to be through a surprising wedding of social and natural sciences in a new forecasting discipline. Though during the early years, the conflicting predictions and underlying power struggle between governmental and private forecasting "baronies" caused some concern, gradually the present reasonably stable state of centralized yet pluralistic forecasting evolved.

Key to this development was the rise of social science to a challenge laid down at its founding by Saint Simon and Comte. While maintaining the advances of particularism, social science leadership managed to transcend the deadly mushrooming of "pigeon-holing" to renew its own bureaucracy. Concepts such as those of psychologist Donald Campbell's "experimenting society,"[2] sociologist Amitai Etzioni's "active society,"[3] futurist Willis Harman's "transindustrial society,"[4] and the rising body of neodialectical thought[5] became rallying points for a tough and persistent band of "amiable revolutionairies." Probably most decisive was their promotion of curriculum changes at both the undergraduate and graduate levels that focused coursework and new majors on the prediction task.

The most controversial element, for a time, was the "foreseeing" aspect of the "foreknowing society." No one in the United States dared to significantly finance research in precognition until the "Psi Papers Scandal" of 1979. When it became known, however, that fresh Soviet successes in grain and other trade negotiations were based on pooling the hunches of teams of "precognizers," congressional pressure forced the National Science Foundation to end the hand-to-mouth existence of obscure projects at Stanford, the Newark College of Engineering, and UCLA with generous funding. Despite widespread use of such "pooling" methods, however, operationally, the academic community is still split over what many call "the mysticism issue."

It is difficult to precisely define the results of moves such as these creating "the foreknowing society." From the perspective of the year 2000, however, it is evident the moves did make differences ranging from facilitating to decisive in the following areas.

The arms race–and particularly the nuclear threat—could easily have done us in if accelerating investments by major powers had not been checked during the 1980s. Some influence here is attributable to a forecasting innovation. This was the use of forecasts, not just of increasing military threats to justify defense increases, but also of socially desired specifics that could be possible *if* defense costs could be checked by *all* major powers. Use of the device by the Carter administration as a friendly challenge to the Soviet government began this movement. World publicity was given by the United States to its annual forecasts of social benefits of this sort that could be available to *Soviet* and other world peoples, as well as to the U.S. populace, and the move seems to have helped encourage some deceleration in arms expenditures.

In checking the growth of a *wasteful and inefficient big government,* forecasting played a decisive role. Here conflict among the forecasting "baronies" had a particularly good effect. Governmental "seers" habitually tried to overforecast benefits and underforecast costs. But the increasing "squawk" power of socially oriented corporate and private forecasting provided a vital counterbalance.

Forecasting did not help much with the major continuing problem of *crime and violence* in general. However, in the specifics of identifying the likely milieus and timing for terrorist acts, forecasts were found very useful by the cooperating antiterrorism world agencies formed during the 1980s.

The *improvement of the U.S. and world environment* was a definite success story for forecasting. Biologist Rachel Carson's *Silent Spring*,[6] the Meadows' group *Limits to Growth,* and a host of other forecasts of environmental disasters kept the public sufficiently aroused to support legislation *and* enforcement with positive effect.

Another area of success was *foreign policy.* In the 1960s forecasting pioneer Bertrand de Jouvenel had felt that a more nearly adequate science could help prevent the "many historical disasters that have been rushed into while the traps were quite visible."[7] This hope came to be, as the U.S. and other forecasting societies developed quicker and more flexible response systems for preventing crises and disasters by anticipating "sensitive events."

The improved response style for foreign policy was prototypical for other areas (e.g., "economic floor" planning) wherein much disruption and dislocation were prevented through anticipation. One important benefit was in *satisfaction with leadership and the political system,* which rose from the low point of Watergate and the Nixon administration to the present healthy balance between acceptance and skepticism. This stability through forecasting may also have affected race relations, for certainly the present higher valuing of racial and all other forms of human diversity seems closely related to the decline in fear and uncertainty about the future of recent years.

It also seems beyond doubt evident that repeated forecasting of the dire consequences of a *dependence on fossil and nuclear fuels* helped begin the crucial phaseout for both these forms and encouraged the development of wind, hydrogen, and solar energy. In overall quality of life, the lessening of alienation and anomie since 1976 are also notable. The first seems an outgrowth of a new feeling for natural systems thinking, eco-mindedness, and community, to some degree attributable to the development of more needs-responsive systems through better forecasting by the private, as well as governmental sectors. The second seems attributable to the feeling prevailing of a concomitant greater social stability.

Finally, the bedrock necessity for the good society—the realization of *love and the stability of marriages and families*—is in possibly the best shape in human history. Forecasting can take some credit here, for warnings of social disaster if the endangered Equal Rights Amendment (ERA) was not passed in 1979 were heeded, and ERA proved to be a crucial turning point for men as well as women in our society.

In short, protected by the advance-warning systems of the foreknowing society, we have passed through the dark times earlier predicted. Both Orwell's *1984* and Huxley's *Brave New World* [9] have so far proved to be chimeras, and the prospect ahead, while far from ideal, is now better than it was earlier.

THE DRIFTING SOCIETY

May I first say I am grateful for the opportunity to write, in secret, smuggling this out, for *The Spit-in-Their-Eye* Newsletter of the Whig-Clio Society at Princeton University.[10] It brings back memories, but words are precious, and so I will not indulge them.

I am deeply saddened, as an old man nearing the end of his time on this earth, to report an overwhelming feeling of ''Once there was Camelot....'' The reference is by now so obscure that I should note, pedantically, that it refers, not to King Arthur, but to the short-lived lift of promise of ''The Kennedy years,'' which, blighted by assassination, unfortunately also foreshadowed the end of the American Dream.

While many factors have contributed to our decline, the one to which I have been hypersensitive was our failure to develop what at one time I called ''the foreknowing society.'' Instead, we are today the hapless captives of that blight upon the still fair face of this earth, ''the drifting society.''

How it all came to be is brutally clear in retrospect. The problem began with the failure of the American people and the American leadership system—consisting of everything from the Jaycees and Senior Chamber of Commerce board members to the so-called ''power elite''—to adequately support the good intentions of two political figures who could have made a difference. The pair were Carter, the suspect southerner, and Mondale, the suspect liberal and ''cryptopinko.'' Under their aegis, moves were made or proposed to bolster governmental forecasting capabilities. They were largely blocked or died, however, as one of many casualties of the resistance of the governmental bureaucracy and its private-sector adherents to Carter's attempt at governmental reorganization.

This failure of the forecasting capability to be realized in government was also mirrored in the private sector, but for other reasons. Here the problem was the refusal of businesses to invest in anything beyond market forecasts for their own products, and the use (or more properly, the *abuse*) by trade associations of the so-called ''impartial'' social forecast as only a self-serving promotional device.

The greatest failure, however, was that of science—and in particular, social science. For a crucial decade—1976 to 1986—leaders and thinkers in every discipline hammered away at their colleagues, trying to bring about more integration and holism and realism of theory and practice. But in the end the compartmentalization feared by Weber in projecting the course of bureaucracy won out. Social science became steadily more a congeries of small ''pet'' practices and theories. Beneath a token facade of ''policy'' research, it was largely run as a sideshow for the benefit of employing teachers and keeping students for six crucial years off the glutted job market. Because forecasting required the integrative, holistic, and realistic orientation, one of many consequences of this unfortunate development was the failure to develop any adequate body of forecasting theory, coursework, or career training.

A related phenomenon I should mention was the rise of a new social science out of natural science. That is, faced with the deficiencies of established social science for their purposes, many socially motivated natural scientists manufactured their own sciences of man. This development was radically accelerated by the growing acceptance of and research into psi abilities by physicists, chemists, biologists, and mathematicians. While social science largely continued to reject the implications of right-brain-half research, several natural scientists produced brilliant integrations of social scientific theory that also incorporated psi phenomena. In the end, however, this possibility for renewal died, for the integrations of the natural scientists were viewed as ''alien invaders'' by the social scientists, who refused to teach or certify them.

The perspective of a near-octogenarian is, of course, largely discredited these days. My views are further discounted as being the suspect grumbling of a potentially still dangerous radical (I look upon this thin hand, this slippered foot, and must laugh!). But I must report that I view these failures as directly relative to the social morass we find ourselves in today. Some items:

War and Defense Expenditures. Rather than forecast and adequately publicize the consequences of war to mankind, all nations, the United States included, used the forecasting of "increasing enemy capabilities" only to promote greater arms expenditures.

Governmental Power. Unchecked by adequate cost–benefit projections, the bureaucracy has grown until even its masters speak openly of a sense of suffocation.

Crime and Violence. Failure even to form a detection and early warning system for terrorism has made of us all players in a giant game of Russian roulette. I am personally riddled with bits of stucco, which are embedded along my right side from the blast that destroyed the apartment house next door and 200 people yesterday. And a son, who is a colonel in the security forces and himself has narrowly escaped such deaths at least 10 times, tells me there are rumors of worse to come. Rumors when there could have been knowledge—and prevention!

The State of Our Environment. This is, however, the bitterest pill to swallow—for so much is endurable if one can have the beauty of nature to gaze upon and have sunshine and clear skies. To think that, spurred by forecasts of disaster, we were well on our way to cleaning and preserving our heritage. But new litterers and vandalizers were born by the increasing billions. Apathetically, our populace has settled back—beer can in hand, watching the equivalent of the Elizabethan bear-baiting on feelavision—to wait for the end.

Foreign Policy. While far from ideal (to put it mildly), today's foreign policy does have a positive aspect. Lacking preventive forecasting, its weekly, and at times daily, crises produce consistently higher Nielsen ratings for the news than for the competing feelavision soap operas. Some may take comfort, then, that this bathing in realism is producing more cognitive gains.

Satisfaction with the System and Leadership.   As we alternate between "strong" and "weak" leadership, it is hard to say which is
worse. There is, of course, satisfaction with neither. Weak leadership,
which avoids our problems, is decried as ineffectual. So-called strong
leadership, which piles up its crude mistakes, is decried as a threat to
freedom (which it is). Lacking forecasting capacities, both are equally
disbelieved.

Energy.   Despite the forecasts that oil would run out and nuclear
reactors could be our ruination, we persisted. Today we live in the
shadow of the authoritarianism forecast by Huxley and Orwell. It has
found its money base in the Arabs—ostensibly to protect their huge
investments in this "unstable" land. Apologists for the nuclear fuel
interests are, of course, saying that the loss of those three cities in Texas
and California is a minor matter compared with the world famine death
rate.

Racial Relations.   The new feudalism is well entrenched, with the
races living each in their own armed enclave. China is the subject of the
day: the rising wonder of the East, which solves these problems inundat-
ing us—and promises the blacks, the browns, and the reds, as well as
the yellow-skinned, it will soon release each each from its ethnic cage,
as our system crumbles and it provides the replacement.

Sexual Relations.   I once knew a love that revealed to me the won-
drous possibilities for social transformation that would derive from an
equality of the sexes. My love wrote her brilliant book, *The Future of
the Sexes,* but its purpose failed and its warnings went unheeded.[11]
Today our couplings are those of robots and the repression of the
feminine in all its aspects poisons beyond description this oppressive
neo-authoritarian state.

This grim fact and the overall drop in the quality of life seem to me,
nearing the end now, worst of all. I think often of the days of my
lake-bound childhood in Minnesota, of youth and early manhood amid
the color and open friendliness of Oklahoma, of the splendor of the
years of myself and beloved family in the intimate and ultimate charm
of Princeton, of the years of a venturing middle life in the sunny embrace of Southern California, and of the resplendent years of love thereafter. It is hard, so hard indeed, to recall those days and look out now

from this detention home for "dangerous radicals" upon the sad or bitter faces of my fellow Americans. Alienation or anomie—it is hard to say which most prevails.[12] Alienation from a system in which everyone of intelligence and feeling feels constrained, a prisoner in social-psychological fact though physically free. Anomie as one shrivels inside with the fear that it is all soon to go down the drain, the foundation crumbled—hence one must clutch to anything and anybody promising even a scrap of stability, no matter how repulsive the bargain that must be struck.

Was this what that glorious man, George Washington, worked for at the outset? May I join his shade soon on "the other side" to marvel and to mourn.

Appendix A
THE IMP QUICK
PREDICTION GUIDE FOR
BUSINESS AND OTHER
ORGANIZATIONAL MANAGERS

This guide is designed to make it possible to apply the theories and findings of Chapters 6, 7, 8, and 9 to some of the practical problems managers face in predicting futures. It is entirely experimental at this stage, and hence its results should be acted on only if they seem to make sense to you intuitively or by any other good rationale. It *is* guaranteed, however, to be better than most forms of unaided guessing, and if applied with ingenuity should considerably sharpen your predictive powers.

I invite anyone who uses this guide to become a participant in a potentially fascinating exercise in practical futures research. Just send a brief writeup of your problem, your analysis, results either pro or con, and any suggestions for modification or improvement to me, care of Wiley-Interscience. If I receive sufficient feedback, this could become the basis for a futures prediction handbook built on *your* case histories. All participants would be credited in the book, of course, unless for any reason you should wish to remain anonymous.

Now for the Guide.

The first thing to do is to examine your problem, or the situation in question, to see if it can be broken down into ''liberal'' versus ''conservative'' positions—or the position of the venturing, more risk-taking ''norm-changers,'' versus the position of the more cautious ''norm-maintainers.'' This basic grounding polarity may be there but at first difficult to see. If so, reread Chapters 6 and 7 to get the feel for this kind of positioning analysis. You may also, however, encounter a problem that simply doesn't lend itself to this kind of analysis—there are many roads to the future. If so, abandon this tack and consider inventing your own approach using the ideas of Chapters 4, 5, and 10 as your guide. (And of course I shall be greatly interested in receiving writeups of all ventures of this sort.)

Now in identifying the basic polarity, let's examine a hypothetical example. Let us say you face the futures prediction problem of deciding on the best site for a new plant or branch office location—or which of two alternative futures look best, town A or town B? Let us further suppose that this question has become an issue within your organization, enlisting strong beliefs and opposing factions in their interpretation of factual research. In such a situation you might identify a "liberal" faction favoring "Risky Town A" versus a "conservative" faction favoring "Safe Town B" To begin your analysis you would state your problem at the top of the form as "Plant Location." (You must do this in a single phrase or sentence to force yourself to begin to compress complexities into simple, useful wholes). Then you would simply write in "Risky Town A" in the slot for the Venturing (A) Position in the attached IMP Quick Prediction Guide, and write in "Safe Town B" in the slot for the Maintaining (B) Position.

Your analysis would then proceed in this way. Carefully observe and mull over the people in the various factions to see how each might align to the subpolarities under each main polarity in terms of convergence versus divergence of opinions. You might find, for example, that among those favoring "Risky Town A" there seemed to be agreement among activists and two inactivists on the issue, and among one who was extreme in his views and two possible moderates. In these instances you would enter a value of 1 in the slot after Activist-Inactivist, and again in the slot after Extreme-Moderate. But then let us say you find disagreements between one particularly tough-minded adherent and three tender-minded sorts, between three "young turks" and one "old guard," and between two who were clearly leaders in this and other situations and two followers. In all three instances you would enter a value of zero to convey a weighting for a lack of consensus, or divergence. Simply totaling these values in the proper slots in the Weightings column (two ones plus three zeros) then gives you a total consensual thrust for the A position of only 2.

As you can see, already you are beginning to articulate a pattern of thrusts that begin to tell you a lot about the Venturing (A) Position. If you follow the same process with the B position and find a Consensual Thrust value of 4, you then subtract 4 from 2 at the bottom of the form and get an IMP Thrust value of minus two (-2). And so you conclude the Maintaining Position will likely prevail for the time being and in the near future. However, if your conclusion is that the total consensual thrust for the B position is absolute zero, then you would have a situation of plus two, minus zero, with plus two remaining as the IMP Thrust. Then you could conclude that, though the Venturing Position thrust was weak, still, for lack of any cohesive opposition, it might very well prevail in the near future.

In all such situations of analysis, it is important to keep in mind that one person can represent several categories—you can have a "leader" who is also "tough-minded" and "extreme." In all such instances, you should, in effect, parcel him out into all three categories—that is, enter him in all three categories because it is the *pattern* of thrusts we are after. In this way, also, you can gain some purchase on future movement with only a handful of people upon whom to base your analysis.

Another question that may be raised is how legitimate is it to try both to fathom a person's position and to estimate convergence or divergences in these categories? Shouldn't you be bolstered with some kind of test or questionnaire? If you want to do this yourself, rather than employ a social scientist, the answer is no. We are each equipped with amazing information-processing and information-categorizing equipment. The best managers learn to use it by forcing themselves to be self-reliant, even when they're protected by large research staffs. If you aren't sufficiently confident to try to categorize your associates and their relationships in the above fashion on your own, without questionnaire support, you shouldn't attempt this exercise—or, for that matter, any kind of futures predicting. You'll be better off employing a consultant futurist.

Consultants and social scientists interested in testing or using this approach will want something more objective than personal assessment, of course. Write me c/o Wiley-Interscience for a copy of the IMP PROFILE, an experimental questionnaire for identifying people according to IMP categories. This measure should prove useful for advanced Delphi studies and evaluations of futurists.

But now, continuing with our example of a plant or office location, what if you find no factional positions developing at home base? What if you find it looks all pretty cut and dried internally, with the statistics lining up clearly for Town A rather than Town B? Then it might be well to look at the communities behind the Town A versus Town B proposed locations. Are there patterns of factional adherence or opposition in these towns that might lend themselves to IMP analysis?

The main point I'm making through this second example is that effective use of the IMP approach will depend on your own ability to gather up some relevant data, get a quick fix on the "gestalt" in terms of potentially meaningful clusterings of beliefs, and so forth, and then use the schema to free your own imagination and guide your own search and analysis.

You might find, for example, that in addition to examining convergences and divergences along the lines for which I've structured the Quick Form here, you also find Ideational Force weightings useful along the lines projected in Chapters 6 and 7. In such cases, having identified the fundamental polarities—and having filled in the A versus B statement slots in the IMP form—you might then proceed to put values into the subcategory "cells," for example, for extremes, moderates, and so on. These values could represent number of adherents to each position. Or they could represent your estimate of special "power thrusts." For example, you might find that the one person you can classify as an extreme is a second vice president, while the one you can classify as a moderate is executive vice president. Obviously the moderate in this case is going to have more power in shaping the decision based on an estimate of future potentials, so you might want to give him a value of 2 against a value of 1 for the other fellow. Or you might even take this matter of weightings a step further and multiply "number of cell adherents" times "power thrust values" to obtain composite IMP cell weightings.

To some, all this will seem ridiculously vague. If so, they really shouldn't bother with this kind of prediction exercise. For of all the creative tasks I have encountered in a fairly long life given over to creativity, futures predicting is not only the most enticing but also the most demanding. The creative person must be able to deal with ambiguities, using them as though the data and the rules for handling it were at first a most diffuse cloud, but progressively, through grappling with the task, gradually imposing one's own forceful sense of relationships upon this cloud. Or to use a better analogy: in space exploration there is an apparatus for improving the clarity of pictures taken by radio telescope of distant stars and planets. The first picture is often fuzzy and hard to follow. But by subjecting it to this computer-aided scanner it is possible to darken, sharpen, and intensify certain patterns, while lightening the spaces in between the darknesses, until an amazingly sharp image of the underlying reality emerges. And this is the important point—that it is a picture of the underlying *reality* rather than a fiction. The same approach—and goal—is possible through using the remarkable powers of the focused human mind. My IMP guide is simply a method of helping to bring about such a useful focusing.

In addition to the IMP Quick Prediction Form, I've attached an IMP Trend Analysis Form. Its purpose is to help add to your powers of prediction by providing a handy means of quantifying repeated IMP samplings. The instructions at the bottom of the form should provide all necessary information for its use and implications.

IMP QUICK PREDICTION FORM

TIME: One _____ (Date:)   Two _____ (Date:)
           Three _____ (Date:)   Four _____ (Date:)

ISSUE, PROBLEM, OR QUESTION: (state in single sentence)

VENTURING (A) POSITION   MAINTAINING (B) POSITION

A CONVERGENCE-DIVERGENCE   B CONVERGENCE-DIVERGENCE
  WEIGHTING   WEIGHTING

Activist-Inactivist   _____   Activist-Inactivist   _____
Extreme-Moderate   _____   Extreme-Moderate   _____
Tough-Tender   _____   Tough-Tender   _____
Older-Younger   _____   Older-Younger   _____
Leader-Follower   _____   Leader-Follower   _____

TOTAL CONSENSUAL THRUST   TOTAL CONSENSUAL THRUST
FOR A POSITION   _____   FOR B POSITION   _____

IMP THRUST: _____ MINUS _____ EQUALS _____
                  A value   B value   IMP Thrust

INSTRUCTIONS: Date your predictions (first through fourth time). State issue, problem, or question in single sentence. State venturing versus maintaining positions. Assign weightings for polarities (activist vs. inactivist, etc.) of 1 for convergence (agreement) or 0 for divergence (lack of agreement). Add up weightings for *A* and for *B*. Insert *A* and *B* values in blanks indicated. Subtract *B* from *A* to get IMP "thrust."

IMP TREND ANALYSIS FORM

ISSUE, PROBLEM, OR QUESTION: _____

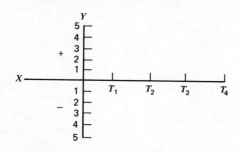

Example of Venturing (*A*)
Future Probability

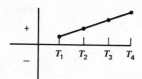

Example of Maintaining (*B*)
Future Probability

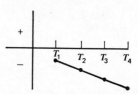

INSTRUCTIONS: Enter IMP thrusts values from IMP Quick Prediction
Forms obtained at Time One (T_1), Time Two (T_2), et cetera, at the
points indicated on the graph. Enter *A* thrusts with <u>plus</u> values
<u>above</u> the *X* axis, *B* thrusts with <u>minus</u> values <u>below</u> the *X* axis.
Examples show how this is done, as well as how this plotting may
show, at a glance, the direction things are headed—or the probable
future.

Appendix B

McGREGOR'S QUESTIONNAIRE

A condensed version of the questionnaire originally printed in the *Journal of Abnormal and Social Psychology*, 1938, **33**:189–209.

1. Will Roosevelt be reelected in November 1936? 86 percent predicted yes.
2. Will Hitler be in power in May 1937? 92 percent predicted yes.
3. Will a major European war be in progress in May 1937? 71 percent predicted no.
4. Will King Edward announce plans for his marriage before May 1937? 58 percent predicted yes.
5. What will be the status of business conditions in May 1937? 70 percent predicted an improvement.
6. Will Lindbergh be living in the United States in May 1937? 57 percent predicted no.
7. What will be the status of the Veterans of Future Wars in May 1937? 57 percent predicted "decline in size and influence."
8. What will be the status of the consumer's cooperative movement in May 1937? 52 percent predicted "increase in size and influence."
9. What will be the approximate membership of the Communist Party of the United States in December 1936? 54 percent predicted between 35,000 and 45,000.

Appendix C

CANTRIL QUESTIONNAIRE, RESULTS, AND HIT-MISS RATING

A condensed version of the questionnaire originally printed on pp. 370–377 of the *Journal of Abnormal and Social Psychology,* 1938, **33.**

1. Do you think President Roosevelt's proposal for the reorganization of the Supreme Court will pass Congress? Yes, 56 percent; no, 44 percent.
2. If you do not think the President's proposal will be adopted, will some compromise plan be passed?
    Yes, 82; no, 18.
3. About what date do you think this issue will be finally settled? 9-1-37, 27 percent; 6-30-37, 22 percent; 6-15-37, 18 percent.
4. Do you think the industrial union, as contrasted to the craft union, will be the predominant type of union in the United States within five years? Yes, 86; no, 14.
5. Do you believe that a strong national Farm-labor party will be formed as a separate party organization by 1940? No, 81; yes, 19.
6. By 1944? No, 54; yes, 46.
7. What party candidate do you think will be elected President in 1940? Democratic, 71; Republican, 21.
8. Do you think all electric power in the United States will at some time be owned and operated by federal, state, or city governments? Yes, 71; no, 29. If "yes," when? 20 years, 38 percent; 40 years, 32 percent; 10 years, 20 percent.
9. Do you think the United States will at some time take over all life insurance? No, 62; yes, 38.
10. Do you think the United States government will at some time own and operate all radio broadcasting? No, 55; yes, 45.
11. Do you think the United States will ever be a collectivized state, comparable to the pattern of Soviet Russia? No, 67; yes, 33. (A majority of yeses said this would happen by 1976.)
12. Do you think the United States will ever have a Fascist dictator on the pattern

of Germany? No, 88; yes, 12. (A majority of yeses said between 1946 and 1956.)

13. Do you think there will be another general European war? Yes, 80; no, 20.

14. If "yes," when will it start? 1941-1945, 28 percent; 1940, 23 percent.

15. Where will it first break out? Central Europe, 39 percent; Ukraine, 25 percent; Spain, 18 percent.

16. How long will it last? 3 years, 32 percent; 2 years, 26 percent; 4–5 years, 13 percent.

17. Who will be the aggressor? Germany, 60 percent; Italy, 28.

18. How will the following nations align themselves? (a) Czechoslovakia, England, France, Poland, U.S.S.R. versus Austria, Germany, Italy, Japan, 56 percent. (b) Czechoslovakia, England, France, U.S.S.R. versus Austria, Germany, Italy, Japan, Poland, 32 percent.

19. Which alignment will win? Czechoslovakia, England, France, Poland, U.S.S.R., 98 percent.

20. Will the United States remain neutral? Only through part of it, 65. Yes, throughout the whole conflict, 27.

21. Which side do you think will win the Spanish Revolution? Loyalists, 51; Rebels, 14.

22. When will this Revolution end? 1937, 58 percent; 1978, 37 percent.

23. What would be the effect of a Rebel victory on the Blum government in France? Weaken it, 40; overthrow it, 28.

24. What would be the effect of a Loyalist victory on the Blum government in France? Strengthen it, 66 percent; no effect, 17 percent.

25. How long do you think the present form of government in Germany will survive? 3–5 years, 43 percent. 6–10 years, 22 percent.

26. If the Nazi government falls, it will be primarily because of: collapse of economic structure, 36; war with a foreign power, 28.

27. If it falls, what form of government will supplant it? Communism, 26. Republic, 24.

28. How long do you think the present form of government in Soviet Russia will survive? Over 150 years, 63 percent.

29. If the Soviet government falls, it will be primarily because of: split within the ruling power, 32. War with a foreign power, 29.

30. Will there be another major depression in the United States? Yes, 95 percent; no, 5.

31. If so, when will it occur? 1943–1950, 46 percent.

32. If so, will there be other depressions following it in future years, or will it be the last one? Others, 88 percent.

33. How long do you think the British Empire will survive in its present form and with its present possessions? Over 150 years, 25 percent.

RATING OF CANTRIL QUESTIONNAIRE RESULTS

1. *Miss*.
2. *Miss*. The court packing bill died in committee.
3. *Hit*. The matter was settled later in the year by Justice Roberts' beginning to vote liberal and Justice Van Devanter's resigning, providing the dependable liberal 5-to-4 vote that FDR sought.
4. *Hit*.
5. *Hit*. Wasn't formed by 1940, as majority predicted.
6. *Hit*. Wasn't formed by 1944, as majority predicted.
7. *Hit*.
8. *Miss*. Hadn't happened by 1956, 20 years after 1936, as majority predicted.
9. *Hit*. Hadn't happened by 1976, as majority who thought it would predicted.
10. *Hit*. Hadn't happened by 1956, as majority who thought it would predicted.
11. *Hit*. Hadn't happened by 1976, as majority who thought it would predicted.
12. *Hit*. Hadn't happened by 1956, as majority who thought it would predicted.
13. *Hit*.
14. *Miss*. Germany invaded Poland, and Britain and France declared war in 1939.
15. Ambiguous. Germany's occupation of Czechoslovakia in March 1929 was central Europe, the majority choice. Germany's invasion of Poland came in September of 1939, a minority choice. Which was the true beginning?
16. *Miss*. The war lasted six years, ending in 1945, rather than the majority choice of three years.
    17.–*Hit*.
18. *Hit*.
19. *Hit*.
20. *Hit*.
21. *Miss*.
22. *Miss*. The Revolution ended in 1939 rather than 1937, as the majority predicted.
23. Meaningless—Blum resigned in 1937, three years before the Franco victory.
24. Ditto.
25. *Miss*. Germany surrendered in 1945, nine years later, rather than within three to five years, the majority prediction.
26. Conditional *hit*. The fall came both because of war and economic collapse, the two main choices.
27. Conditional *hit*. East Germany became Communist, West Germany became a Republic.
28. Unratable.
29. *Miss*.
30. *Miss*.

Score: 16 hits out of 26 ratable predictions, or 62 percent.

Appendix D

TABLES FOR THE 1972 PRINCETON STUDY

TABLE D.1   Content of Conflict Issues

1. WAR AND DEFENSE

Liberal concerns	%	Conservative concerns	%
War		*War*	
Extremes: Actualities of Viet Nam war and the draft.	30* (7)	Extremes: Left's Marxist exploitation of war as issue.	20 (2)
Moderates: Actualities of Viet Nam war and the draft.	35 (8)	Moderates: Irrationality of call for immediate U.S. withdrawal.	11 (2)
Defense		*Defense*	
Extremes: Arms race, too much military spending, against ROTC.	17 (4)	Extremes: Rapid decline in military superiority over Russians; should spend $20 billion more yearly and cut back welfare; for ROTC.	40 (4)
Moderates: Military spending, nuclear doomsday threat, against ROTC.	26 (6)	Moderates: Declining defense posture; deterioration in U.S.–Russian balance of power; for ROTC.	44 (8)

2. GOVERNMENT AS SOCIAL MECHANISM

liberal concerns	%	Conservative concerns	%
Extremes: nonresponsive at all levels to needs of the people; poor ordering of priorities; hypocrisy, lack of social candor.	22 (5)	Extremes: Public support of governmental paternalism (e.g., Family Assistance Program).	20 (2)
		Moderates: centralized at-	33

Moderates: dishonesty in government; lack of trust in government; hypocrisy; service of special interests; failure of big government to respond to masses.

22

(5)

tempts to solve social problems; cutback in NASA; excessive regulation, from FDA to ICC; interference of government with Lockheed and other industries; United States too much of a welfare state.

(6)

In Tables D.1, D.2, and D.3, for each category the primary number is an indication of concern on the issue figured as a percentage of total expressions of concern; the number in parentheses below it is the number of respondents per issue, by ideology. For example, beginning Table D.1, of the total number of expressions of concern about the Vietnam War, 30 percent were by extreme liberals, 7 in number; 35 percent were by moderate liberals, 8 in number; 20 percent by extreme conservatives 2 in number; and 11 percent by moderate conservatives, 2 in number. Percentages are number of expressions per issue per category divided by the number of respondents in the category. As some respondents expressed more than one concern regarding the category, this results in a few percentages larger than 100. This looks peculiar, but is a better indicator than the number of expressions per category divided by total number of expressions per category, which would result in all percentages less than 100, but would distort findings because of inequal Ns.

TABLE D.2   Content of Consensus Issues

1.CRIME AND VIOLENCE

Liberal concerns	%	Conservative concerns	%
Extremes: Escalation of antihuman violence everywhere; ineffectiveness of prison system.	17 (4)	Extremes: Violence; lack of discipline on campus; weakening of rules to allow savage behavior; Warren Court distorts Constitution; courts should be more severe with those convicted of serious crimes.	90 (9)
Moderates: Crime; shooting of policemen; need for law and order, gun control, more personal security; life should not be hounded by the fear of capricious violence.	35 (8)	Moderates: Crime is the major problem of our society; tearing down of standards without replacing them; ineffectiveness of prison system; log jam in courts; excessive leniency toward criminals.	33 (6)

2. ENVIRONMENT

Extremes: Ecology; destruction of wildlife and natural resources; oppressive environment of cities.	22 (5)	Extremes: No comments.	0 (0)
Moderates: Lack of concern for ecology; lack of concern by Nixon administration for urban slums; urban blight; banal cultural fare on TV.	57 (13)	Moderates: Unwillingness of business and common man to preserve ecology; selling out to polluters; irreparable damage of strip mining; not enough tax money spent on pollution control; lack of effective urban renewal; urban plight; TV news bias.	56 (10)

3. GOVERNMENTAL POWER

Extremes: No comments.	0 (0)	Extremes: Encroachment on individual freedom; slow movement of the country toward more gun controls and socialism.	20 (2)
Moderates: Overloaded bureaucracy; disorganization and inefficiency of governmental policy; state–city relations; state–religion relation; spending for interstate highways.	22 (5)	Moderates: Bureaucracy; growth in government; growing encroachment on state, local, individual rights and power.	17 (3)

4. TAXES

Extremes: Taxes, no comment.	4 (1)	Extremes: Burdensome and graduated taxes.	10 (1)
Moderates: High taxes "and other monetary ripoffs"; need for tax reform.	13 (3)	Moderates: Growth in, especially property taxes; wasted tax revenues.	17 (3)

TABLE D.3   Content of Mixed Issues

1. FOREIGN POLICY

Liberal concerns	%	Conservative concerns	%
Extremes: American foreign policy as a major area of concern (23 expressions); Russian	104 (24)	Extremes: American foreign policy as a major area of concern (10 expressions);	100 (10)

and Arab threat to Israel (1).

Moderates: U.S. exploitation　13
of third-world countries; plight　(3)
of Bangladesh.

Taiwan's autonomy must be
preserved (1).

Moderates: American foreign　127
policy as a major area of con-　(23)
cern (18 expressions).
Isolationist wave in U.S., inept
foreign policy, lack of U.S.
reaction to Soviet penetration
of Mediterranean and Indian
Oceans, U.S.–Canadian relations, U.S. relations with India
and Pakistan.

2. POLITICAL SYSTEM AND LEADERSHIP

general dissatisfaction
Extremes: Dissatisfaction with　17
two-party system; with system　(4)
based on self-interests of individuals fraudulently rep-
resented as the "will of the
people"; with misinformation
given by political leadership;
actions that ignore causes of
real problems and inefficiently
attack effects.

Moderates: Cynicism and　22
negativism of many young　(5)
people toward political apparatus needed for social
change; monetary waste of
party politics; money in politics; lack of commitment to ending our problems; constraints
on leaders due to pressures.

General dissatisfaction
Extremes: No comments.　　　0

Moderates: No comments.　　　0

Polarization
Extremes: Polarization in na-　13
tion; lack of intelligent discus-　(3)
sion by those flinging epithets;
George Wallace plays on fears
of people.

Polarization
Extremes: Weakness of Liberal　60
Establishment allowing left to　(6)
radicalize population; abundance liberal professors; glos-
sing over of moderate and con-

Moderates: Wallace divides an already fragmented country. 4 (1)

servative views; liberal bias promoted by profs; left-wing attitude that it owns truth and desire to suppress conservative speakers; absolutist thinking; inability to distinguish relatives from absolutes.

Moderates: Polarization of students into right and left factions, leaving little ground for middle; curbing freedom of speech nationally as well as on campus; exert mind-control on vast numbers of students; possibility that freedom of speech will be overcome by liberal bias in universities; foolish and intellectually emasculating habit of labeling one's self either "liberal" or "conservative." 55 10)

Nixon

Extremes: No comments. 0

Moderates: Nixon backtracking on busing; slowness to fight heroin traffic; unconcern with urban slums; problems in general; aristocratic types are callously Nixonian; economic policy; lack of concern for blacks; stand on busing; everything about him. "I cannot in my lifetime see a President whom I could trust; the possibility that no man in that office can hold the trust of the people is very disturbing." 35 (8)

Nixon

Extremes: Policy of building bridges to our enemies; failure to challenge liberal preconceptions; his liberal policies. 30 (3)

Moderates: Need to reelect Nixon; dishonesty in politics—Integrity, campaign spending, ITT, Carswell, etc. "Only turning to the leadership of Jesus Christ can give us peace, justice or love in the world. Until this occurs man's efforts are of little value." 22 (4)

3. RACE

Extremes: Racism; lack of progress on Civil Rights; 48 (11)

Extremes: Reverse discrimination in university admission 20 (2)

174 THE KNOWABLE FUTURE

amount of prejudice; Nixon busing plan a farce and sellout; hypocrites who claim quality education can't happen in segregated schools; Jewish quota on campus; polarization of blacks and whites on campus.

Moderates: Racism; bigotry; busing, Civil Rights; oppose Nixon stand on busing; students who talk of campus niggers, Wallace is liked by some; possibilities of race war; polarization of blacks and whites on campus.

61
(14)

policies; people seem to feel law can bring about racial harmony, laws only produce resentment that hurts relations; true harmony is personal and must come from deep inside.

Moderates: Relaxing entrance standards for "various groups of applicants to P.U."; forced integration; school busing as a means of achieving integration; government can't solve problem, only individuals who have turned to Jesus; Jewish quota on campus; rise in both black and white racism; racial polarization on campus.

44
(8)

REFERENCE NOTES

Chapter 1

1. Of the ancient texts I have examined, *I Ching* is by far the most interesting from the viewpoint of futures prediction through both conscious and unconscious mind. Its classification as a work of convoluted necromancy has obscured a highly sophisticated system for futures prediction based entirely on the use of patterns of change observable through use of *conscious* mind. The best text is *The I Ching, or Book of Changes* published by the Princeton University Press, with foreword by Carl Jung. A highly useful supplementary text is John Blofeld's translation and commentary published by Dutton.

2. The sources I have used for the Adams' family material are, to a slight extent, *The Education of Henry Adams,* and to a much greater extent, *The Degradation of Democratic Dogma.* In this last book, which contains Adams' key essay on phases, the long introduction by Brooks Adams is an invaluable source of historical information.

3. *Degradation of Democratic Dogma,* p. 23.

4. *Ibid,* p. 32.

5. *Ibid,* p. 84.

6. *Ibid,* p. 98.

7. For a summary of the work of Ridenour, Price, Rappaport, and others relating to Adams' earlier speculations, see Bell, D. "Twelve Modes of Prediction."

8. *Degradation of Democratic Dogma,* p. 309.

9. *Kahn and Weiner, The Year 2000.*

10. Helmer, *Social Technology.*

11. De Jouvenel, *The Art of Conjecture.*

12. Bell, *Toward the Year 2000.*

13. Meadows et al., *The Limits to Growth;* Mesarovic and Pestel, *Mankind at the Turning Point.*

14. Harman, "The Coming Transformation."

15. Drucker, *The Age of Discontinuity.*

16. In contrast to the 25,000 members of the American Economic Association and the 14,000 members of the American Sociological Association, in

1976 the American Psychological Association had 39,000 members, the American Psychiatric Association, 21,000.
17. Michael, *The Future Society.*
18. London, "The Problem of Contemporary Analysis in History and Psychology."
19. Toch, "The Perception of Future Events."
20. Osgood and Umpleby, "A Computer-Based System for Exploration of Possible Futures for Mankind 2000."
21. Rokeach, *The Nature of Human Values.*
22. Mankin, *Toward a Post-Industrial Psychology.*
23. Goodman, *The Future and the Human Brain.*
24. Progoff, *Jung, Synchronicity, and Human Destiny.*
25. McCully, "The Rorschach, Synchronicity, and Relativity."
26. Gorney, *The Human Agenda.*
27. McClelland, *The Achieving Society.*
28. McGregor, "The Major Determinants of the Prediction of Social Events."
29. Cantril, "The Prediction of Social Events."
30. Gallup, *The Miracle Ahead.*
31. McGregor, *The Human Side of Enterprise.*
32. Cantril, "The Human Design."
33. McClelland, *The Achieving Society.*
34. See bibliography for a fascinating followup to another "forgotten" study by Cantril, Hans Toch's "The Perception of Future Events."

Chapter 2

1. De Jouvenel, *The Art of Conjecture,* p. viii.
2. *Ibid,* p. 28.
3. *Ibid,* p. 29.
4. *Ibid,* pp. 37, 38.
5. Henle, *Documents of Gestalt Psychology.*
6. Lewin, *Field Theory in Social Science.*
7. Kahn and Weiner, *The Year 2000.*
8. Kahn and Briggs, *Things to Come.*
9. Kahn, in *The Futurist,* p. 286.
10. Mill, *Principles of Political Economy.*
11. Marx, *Economic and Philosophic Manuscripts of 1844.*
12. Mumford, *The Condition of Man.*
13. Sorokin, *Social and Cultural Dynamics.*
14. Kahn, *The Year 2000,* p. 189. Here Kahn's referent is the Emperor Augustus, whose reign was a notable high point of stability for the Roman Empire. Elsewhere he speaks of "Augustinian" versus "Pelagian" views of man, but in this case the referent is Saint Augustine, Bishop of Hippo.
15. Helmer, *Social Technology.*

16. Helmer, "An Agenda for Futures Research."
17. Peccei, *Mankind at the Turning Point,* p. 206.
18. *Ibid.*

Chapter 3

1. Messarovic and Pestel, *Mankind at the Turning Point,* p. 34.
2. De Jouvenel, *The Art of Conjecture,* p. 38.
3. This only scratches the surface of a dissatisfaction with present paradigms and results of social science mounting among its practitioners, for example, Elms' "The Crisis of Confidence in Social Psychology"; Smith, "Is Psychology Relevant to New Priorities?"; Carlson, "Where is the Person in Personality Research?"; Gouldner, "The Coming Crisis of Western Sociology"; Roberts, "On the Nature and Condition of Social Science."
4. A good summary of old and more recent self-psychologies is Hall and Lindzey's *Theories of Personality.*
5. See Ittelson and Cantril, *Perception, a Transactional Approach;* Tagiuri, *Perception and Interpersonal Behavior.*
6. Ames, *Morning Notes.*
7. De Jouvenel, *The Art of Conjecture,* p. 74.
8. *Ibid,* p. 118.
9. Besides *A Dynamic Theory of Personality* by Lewin, good sources on Lewin include Hall and Lindzey's *Theories of Personality;* Deutsch and Krauss, *Theories in Social Psychology;* and Loye, *The Healing of a Nation,* Chapters 25 and 26.
10. De Jouvenel, *The Art of Conjecture,* p. 126.
11. Loye, *The Healing of a Nation.*
12. Kahn, *The Year 2000.*
13. Lewin, Lippitt, and White, *Autocracy and Democracy: An Experimental Inquiry.* Also Loye, *The Healing of a Nation,* pp. 291–295, 319–320.
14. Kahn, *The Next 200 Years,* p. 193.
15. Maslow, *Toward a Psychology of Being.*
16. Riegel, "Time and Change in the Development of the Individual and Society."
17. Bronfenbrenner, *Two Worlds of Childhood.*
18. Messarovic and Pestel, p. 43.
19. *Ibid,* p. 54.
20. McGuire, "The Nature of Attitude and Attitude Change."
21. Rokeach, *The Nature of Human Values.*
22. Mesarovic and Pestel, p. 146.
23. Deutsch, "Cooperation and Trust: Some Theoretical Notes."
24. Sherif, "Experiments in Group Conflict."
25. Osgood, *An .Alternative to War or Surrender.*
26. Messarovic and Pestel.

27. Jung, *Modern Man in Search of a Soul.*
28. Erikson, *Identity: Youth and Crisis.*
29. Fromm, *Man for Himself.*
30. Lewin, *Resolving Social Conflicts.*
31. Maslow, *Toward a Psychology of Being.*
32. De Jouvenel, p. 108.
33. *Ibid,* p. 113.
34. *Ibid,* p. 240.
35. *Ibid,* p. 240.
36. *Ibid,* p. 254.
37. *Ibid,* p. 255.
38. Kahn, *Things to Come,* pp. 82, 83.
39. *Ibid,* p. 96.
40. *Ibid,* p. 246.
41. *Ibid,* p. 246.
42. *Ibid,* p. 247.
43. Mesarovic and Pestel, p. 151.

Chapter 4

1. Fechner, "Elements of Psychophysics."
2. Blumenthal, "A Reappraisal of Wilhelm Wundt," p. 1086.
3. James, *The Principles of Psychology,* I, pp. 288–289.
4. Thibault and Kelley, *Social Psychology of Groups.*
5. Larsson, *Bayes Strategies and Human Information Seeking.*
6. Sherif, *The Psychology of Social Norms.*
7. Hamilton, "Personality Attributes Associated with Extreme Response Style."
8. Fishbein, *The Intuitive Sources of Probabilistic Thinking in Children.*
9. Brehm and Cohen, *Explorations in Cognitive Dissonance.*
10. Westcott, *Toward a Contemporary Psychology of Intuition.*
11. An excellent summary of the above and other psychological works relevant to futures studies is *Toward a Post-Industrial Psychology* by Don Mankin.
12. Miller, Gallanter, and Pribram, *Plans and the Structure of Behavior.*
13. Wooldridge, *The Machinery of the Brain.*
14. Ornstein, *The Psychology of Consciousness.*
15. *Ibid,* pp. 66, 68.
16. *Ibid,* pp. 92, 93.
17. Piaget, *The Psychology of Intelligence.*
18. Skinner, *Verbal Behavior.*
19. Bruner, Goodnow, and Austin, *A Study of Thinking.*
20. Berlyne, *Conflict, Arousal, and Curiosity.*
21. Kohler, *The Mentality of Apes.*
22. McGregor, "Determinants of Prediction of Social Events," p. 180.

23. Freud, *An Outline of Psychoanalysis*.
24. Bruner, "The Conditions of Creativity."
25. McGregor, p. 197.
26. Tomkins, "The Psychology of Knowledge."
27. Loye, *The Leadership Passion: A Psychology of Ideology*.
28. Cantril, "The Prediction of Social Events."
29. Katona, "Fifteen Years of Experience with Measurement of Consumer Expectations."
30. Gallup, *The Gallup Poll, Public Opinion: 1935–1971*.
31. Various successful experiments using "citizen feedback" concepts have been conducted by Loren Halvorsen of the Lutheran Church, Stuart Umpleby and associates at the University of Illinois, economist Robert Theobald, Mike McManus working with New York's Regional Planning Association and the Gallup Organization, and many others. A projection of the dramatic possibilities for such work in futures interventions is outlined in the last chapter of Loye, *The Healing of a Nation*.
32. Watts and Free, *State of the Nation*.
33. Sheldon and Moore, *Indicators of Social Change: Concepts and Measurements*.
34. McGregor, pp. 201, 202.
35. Helmer, "An Agenda for Futures Research."
36. Kaplan, Skogstad, and Gershick, "The Prediction of Social and Technological Events."
37. Lewin, Lippitt, and White, *Autocracy and Democracy*.
38. Kaplan, Skogstad, and Gershick, "The Prediction of Social and Technological Events."
39. Turoff, "Delphi Conferencing: Computer-based Conferencing with Anonymity."
40. Dalkey, "The Delphi Method: An Experimental Study of Group Opinion."
41. Fincher, *Human Intelligence*.
42. Sackman, *Delphi Critique*. The reader should be warned this is a warped and savagely biased critique of Delphi methods.
43. Helmer, Appendix to *Social Technology*.
44. Gallup, *The Gallup Poll, Public Opinion 1935–1971*.
45. Cantril, p. 365.
46. McGregor, p. 202.

Chapter 5

1. Ornstein, *The Psychology of Consciousness*, p. 113.
2. Freud, *Interpretation of Dreams*.
3. Jung, *Memories, Dreams and Reflections*.
4. Pratt, *Parapsychology: An Insider's View of ESP*.

5. Moss, *The Probability of the Impossible,* pp. 209–211.
6. Hall and Lindzey, *Theories of Personality.*
7. Murphy, *The Challenge of Psychical Research.*
8. Brier and Tyminski, "Psi Applications: Parts I and II."
9. Krippner, Ullman, and Vaughan, *Dream Telepathy.*
10. Moss, *The Probability of the Impossible.*
11. Targ and Puthoff, *Mind-Reach,* p. 116.
12. Dean, Mihalasky, Ostrander, and Schroeder, *Executive ESP.*
13. Schmeidler, "Precognition Scores Related to the Subject's Ways of Viewing Time."
14. Greeley, *The Sociology of the Paranormal: A Reconnaissance.*
15. Taff, "Learned PSI: An Exploration of Parameters in a Controlled Study."
16. Moss, *The Probability of the Impossible.*
17. Vaughan, *Patterns of Prophecy.*
18. *Ibid.*
19. *Ibid.*
20. *Ibid.*
21. *Ibid.*
22. Koestler, *The Roots of Coincidence.*
23. *Ibid;* Ostrander and Schroeder, *Psychic Discoveries behind the Iron Curtain.*
24. Henle, *Basic Documents of Gestalt Psychology.*
25. Lewin, *A Dynamic Theory of Personality.*
26. Moss, *The Probability of the Impossible.*
27. *Ibid.*
28. Pehek, Kyler, and Faust, "Image Modulation in Corona Discharge Photography."
29. Puthoff and Targ, "Psychical Phenomena and Modern Physics."
30. Vaughan, *Patterns of Prophecy.*
31. Loye, *Journey into a Pocket Utopia.* A work in progress.
32. Taff, "A Memory of Things to Come"; "Brain Holograms: The Light Within."
33. These informal experiments involved Barry Taff, Kerry Gaynor, Steve Greenebaum, and myself. see Loye, *Adventures of a Sunday Psychic.*
34. Vaughan, *Patterns of Prophecy.*
35. Mihalasky, "An Improved Delphi Method of Group Decision Making: Report on a Research Grant."
36. Mihalasky in *Executive ESP,* p. 152.

Chapter 6

1. Woolman and Birney forecasts and sources are outlined in Loye, *The Healing of a Nation.*
2. Flexner, *Washington: The Indispensable Man.*

3. Adams, B. Introduction to *Degradation of Democratic Dogma,* pp. 17–19.
4. Sherif, "The Relevance of Social Psychology."
5. Loye, *The Leadership Passion,* chapters 2, 3, and 14.
6. Loye, *The Healing of a Nation,* Chapter 12.
7. Michael, Letter to the Editor, *APA Monitor,* March 1977, p. 27.
8. Loye, *The Leadership Passion,* Part IV.
9. Boocock and Schild, *Simulation Games in Learning.*
10. De Jouvenel, p. 39.
11. Eysenck, *The Psychology of Politics.*
12. Cattell, *The Scientific Analysis of Personality.*
13. Comrey, *Comrey Personality Scales.*
14. Loye, *The Leadership Passion.*
15. Packard, *The Status Seekers;* Bell, *Post-Industrial Society.*
16. Schlesinger, "The Tides of Politics."
17. Young, *The Rise of the Meritocracy;* Vonnegut, *Player Piano.* I predict that within 10 to 20 years it will become generally evident that Vonnegut, as a writer free to intuit beyond science's contemporary "prison," was in this and later books dealing with a surprising range of advanced issues for both "hard" and "soft" science.
18. Loye, *The Leadership Passion.*
19. Those interested in advancing this theory should examine articles dealing with convergence and divergence by Ivan London listed in my bibliography. Langmuir's view as presented by Dr. London is both similar to and different from the approach I take, but the fact the end practical goal is the same should make London's papers invaluable to anyone wanting to go beyond what I present in theory building.

Chapter 7

1. Historians who reviewed chapters relevant to their interests prior to publication included John Hope Franklin, C. Vann Woodward, Martin Duberman, Eric Goldman, Benjamin Quarles, Philip Foner, David Brion Davis, and Saunders Redding. The book received the Anisfield–Wolfe Award for the best scholarly book on race relations in 1971 from a committee including historian Oscar Handlin.
2. Kahn, *The Year 2000,* p. 26.
3. Loye, *The Healing of a Nation,* Chapter 4.
4. This phenomenon will be explored in depth in my work in progress, *The Psychology of the Middle.*
5. Loye, *The Healing of a Nation,* Chapter 11.
6. *Ibid,* p. 108.
7. Theobald, *Futures Conditional.*

Chapter 8

1. This instrument and results will be described in *The Psychology of the Middle*.
2. These groups are portrayed in depth in Part III of *The Leadership Passion*.
3. Parsons and Shils, *Theories of Society*.

Chapter 9

1. Loye, Gorney, and Steele, "Television Effects: An Experimental Field Study."

Chapter 10

1. Comte, quoted by de Jouvenel, *The Art of Conjecture*, p. 111.
2. *Ibid,* p. 101
3. De Jouvenel, *Power, and The Pure Theory of Politics*.
4. Good definitions of the neglected factor of ideation may be found in Cassirer, "Ideational Contents of the Sign," and Tomkins, "The Psychology of Knowledge."
5. Weber, "The Social Psychology of the World Religions," *The Protestant Ethic*. To my knowledge, the term *institutional press* is not Weberian but simply my term representing an extension of ideational press into the social context.
6. Riegel, "Manifesto for a Dialectical Psychology."
7. Adams, *Degradation of Democratic Dogma,* p. 38.
8. *Ibid,* p. 107.
9. A leading journal for futurism is *Technological Forecasting and Social Change*.
10. Heisenberg, *Physics and Philosophy*.
11. Kahn and Weiner, *The Year 2000*.
12. Harman, "The Coming Transformation."
13. Kant, *Critique of Pure Reason*.
14. Adams, *The Degradation of Democratic Dogma,* p. 95.
15. It is interesting to note that my expression here of a kind of "leap" is very much like the postulations of early Gestalt thinkers regarding the operation of insight in conscious problem-solving. A major theoretical battle of the 1920s, 1930s, and into the 1940s, was then between the gestaltists and the behaviorists, who asserted there was no such leap, only a series of associational links collapsed by repetition into the *appearance* of a leap.
16. Among sources articulating this "separate reality" is, of course, the work by Carlos Castenada by this title, *A Separate Reality*.
17. Adams, *Degradation of Democratic Dogma,* p. 38.
18. Taff, "Learned PSI: An Exploration of Parameters in a Controlled Study."
19. Moss, *The Probability of the Impossible*.

20. Taff, "Learned PSI."
21. Dean and Mihalasky, *Executive ESP*.
22. Greeley, *The Sociology of the Paranormal*.
23. Heisenberg, quote from Koestler, *The Roots of Coincidence,* p. 51.
24. This view, which on the face of it suggests the alien cultural "exoticism," Eastern religion and philosophy, is also firmly rooted in the Western tradition. It occurs, for example, in Plato, in the visionary perceptions of William Blake ("To see a world in a grain of sand/And a heaven in a wild flower/ Hold infinity in the palm of your hand/and eternity in an hour,") in Kant's philosophy, and in the speculations of modern physicists and mathematicians, as detailed by Arthur Koestler in *The Roots of Coincidence* and *The Challenge of Chance*. Within the context of precognition studies, Taff is an ardent advocate of this view in papers such as "It's About Time" and "A Memory of Things to Come."
25. Goodman, *The Future and the Human Brain*.
26. Goodman, "Learning from Lobotomy."
27. Luria, *The Working Brain*.
28. Miller, Gallanter, and Pribram. *Plans and the Structure of Behavior*.
29. Koestler, *The Roots of Coincidence*.
30. LEWIN, *The Dynamic Theory of Personality* and *Field Theory in Social Science*.
31. Freud, *Complete Introductory Lectures in Psychoanalysis*.
32. Weber, *The Social Psychology of the World's Religions*.
33. Plato, *The Republic*, Chapter 25.
34. Paul, *The Bible,* first letter to the Corinthians.
35. Schroeder, "The View from All Over."
36. Taff, "A Memory of Things to Come."
37. Adams, *Degradation of Democratic Dogma,* p. 310.
38. Progoff, *Jung, Synchronicity, and Human Destiny*.
39. De Jouvenel, p. 88.
40. De Jouvenel, correspondence with author, June 5, 1976.
41. De Jouvenel, *The Art of Conjecture,* p. 277.

Chapter 11

1. Fuller, *Utopia or Oblivion*. Others who have played the visionary role in many books include economists Robert Theobald, Robert Heilbroner, and Kenneth Boulding; psychoanalysts Erich Fromm and Roderic Gorney; generalist Lewis Mumford and George Leonard; writers Aldous Huxley and George Orwell.
2. Campbell, "The Social Scientist as Methodological Servant of the Experimenting Society."
3. Etzioni, *The Active Society*.
4. Harman, "The Coming Transformation."

5. Riegel, "A Manifesto for Dialectical Psychology."
6. Carson, *Silent Spring*.
7. Correspondence with author, April 5, 1976.
8. Orwell, *1984*.
9. Huxley, *Brave New World*.
10. The Whig-Clio Society and my past association are described in Loye, *The Leadership Passion*.
11. Eisler, *The Future of the Sexes*.
12. Alienation and anomie are redefined in terms of a new theoretical structure for ideology in Loye, *The Leadership Passion*.

REFERENCES

Adams, H. *The degradation of democratic dogma*. New York: MacMillan, 1920.

Adams, H. *The education of Henry Adams*. Boston, Mass.: Houghton-Mifflin, 1961.

Bell, D. *The coming of post-industrial society*. New York: Basic, 1973.

Bell, D. (Ed.). *Toward the year 2000: work in progress. Boston, Mass.: Beacon, 1969.*

Bell, D. *"Twelve modes of prediction."* Daedalus, 1964, **93**:845–880.

Berlyne, D. *Conflict, arousal, and curiosity*. New York: McGraw-Hill, 1960.

Blumenthal, A. "A reappraisal of Wilhelm Wundt." *American Psychologist*, 1975, **30**(11):1081–1088.

Boocock, S., and Schild, E. (Eds.). *Simulation games in learning*. Beverly Hills, Calif.: Sage Publications, 1968.

Boucher, W. (Ed.) *The study of the future: an agenda for research*. National Science Foundation, 1977.

Brehm, J., and Cohen, A. *Explorations in cognitive dissonance*. New York: Wiley, 1962.

Brier, R., and Tyminski, W. "Psi applications: parts I and II." *Journal of Parapsychology,* 1970, **34**:1–36.

Bronfenbrenner, U. *Two worlds of childhood*. New York: Russell Sage, 1970.

Bruner, J. "The conditions of creativity." In H. Gruber, G. Terrell, and M. Wertheimer (Eds.). *Contemporary approaches to creative thinking*. New York: Atherton, 1962.

Bruner, J., Goodnow, J., and Austin, G. *A study of thinking*. New York: Wiley, 1956.

Campbell, D. "The social scientist as methodological servant of the experimenting society." *Policy Studies Journal,* 1973, **2**:72–75.

Cantril, H. "The human design." In E. Hollander and R. Hunt (Eds.). *Current perspectives in social psychology*. New York: Oxford University Press, 1967.

Cantril, H. "The prediction of social events." *Journal of Abnormal and Social Psychology,* 1938, **33**:364–389.

Carlson, R. "Where is the person in personality research?" *Psychological Bulletin,* 1971, **75**:203–219.

Carson, R. *Silent spring*. Boston, Mass.: Houghton-Mifflin, 1962.

Cassirer, E. "Ideational contents of the sign." In T. Parsons et al. (Eds.). *Theories of society*. New York: Free Press, 1961.

Casteneda, C. *A separate reality*. New York: Simon & Schuster, 1971.

Cattell, R. *The scientific analysis of personality*. Baltimore: Penguin, 1965.

Comrey, A. *Comrey personality scales*. San Diego, Calif.: Educational and Industrial Testing Service, 1970.

Cornish, E. *The study of the future: an introduction to the art and science of understanding and shaping tomorrow's world*. Washington, D.C.: World Future Society, 1977.

Dalkey, N. (Ed.). *Studies in the quality of life: Delphi and decision making.* Lexington, Mass.: Heath, 1972.

Dean, D., Mihalasky, J., Ostrander, S., and Schroeder, L. *Executive ESP.* Englewood Cliffs, N.J.: Prentice-Hall, 1974.

De Jouvenel, B., *On power.* New York: Viking, 1949.

De Jouvenel, B. *The art of conjecture.* New York: Basic Books, 1967.

De Jouvenel, B. *The pure theory of politics.* New Haven, Conn.: Yale University Press, 1963.

Deutsch, M. "Cooperation and trust: some theoretical notes." In M. Jones (Ed.). *Nebraska Symposium on Motivation, 1962.* Lincoln, Nebraska: University of Nebraska Press, 1962, pp. 275–318.

Deutsch, M., and Krauss, R. *Theories in social psychology.* New York: Basic Books, 1965.

Drucker, P. *The age of discontinuity.* New York: Harper & Row, 1969.

Eisler, R. *The future of the sexes.* Work in progress, 1977.

Eisler, R. *The sex rights handbook.* New York: Avon, 1978.

Elms, A. "The crisis of confidence in social psychology." *American Psychologist,* 1975, **30**(10):967–976.

Erikson, E. *Identity: youth and crisis.* New York: Norton, 1968.

Etzioni, A. *The active society.* New York: Free Press, 1968.

Eysenck, H. *The psychology of politics.* London: Routledge and Kegan Paul, 1954.

Fechner, G. "Elements of psychophysics." In W. Dennis (Ed.). *Readings in the history of psychology.* New York: Appleton-Century-Crofts, 1948.

Fincher, J. *Human intelligence.* New York: Putnam, 1976.

Fishbein, E. *The intuitive sources of probabilistic thinking in children.* Boston, Mass.: Reidel, 1975.

Flexner, J. *Washington: the indispensable man.* Boston, Mass.: Little, Brown, 1974.

Freud, S. *Complete introductory lectures in psychoanalysis.* New York: Norton, 1966.

Freud, S. *An outline of psychoanalysis.* New York: Norton, 1970.

Freud, S. *Interpretation of dreams.* New York: Modern Library, 1950.

Fromm, E. *Man for himself.* Holt, Rinehart & Winston, 1947.

Fuller, B. *Utopia or oblivion: the prospects for humanity.* New York: Bantam, 1969.

Gallup, G. *The Gallup poll, public opinion: 1935–1971.* New York: Random House, 1972.

Gallup, G. *The miracle ahead.* New York: Harper & Row, 1966.

Gilfillan, S. "A sociologist looks at technical prediction." In J. Bright (Ed.). *Technological forecasting for industry and government: method and applications.* Englewood Cliffs, N.J.: Prentice-Hall, 1968.

Goldschmidt, P. "Scientific inquiry or political critique? Remarks on Delphi assessment by H. Sackman." *Technological Forecasting and Social Change,* 1975, **7**:195–213.

Goodman, D. *The future of the human brain.* Work in progress.

Goodman, D. "Learning from lobotomy: a study of the transformation of human intelligence." *Human Behavior,* January, 1978.

Gorney, R. *The human agenda.* New York: Simon & Schuster, 1972.

Gouldner, *The coming crisis of western sociology.* New York: Basic Books, 1970.

Greeley, A. *The sociology of the paranormal: a reconnaissance.* Beverly Hills, Calif.: Sage, 1975.

Hall, C., and Lindzey, G. *Theories of personality*. New York: Wiley, 1970.

Hamilton, D. "Personality attributes associated with extreme response style." *Psychological Bulletin, 1968,* **69**(3):192–203.

Hardy, A., Harvie, R., and Koestler, A. *The challenge of chance*. New York: Random House, 1973.

Harman, W. "The coming transformation, parts I and II." *The Futurist,* 1977, **1**(11):4–12, and **2**:106–112.

Harman, W. *An incomplete guide to the future*. San Francisco, Calif.: San Francisco Book Co., 1976.

Heisenberg, W. *Physics and philosophy*. New York: Harper & Row, 1958.

Helmer, O. "*An agenda for futures research.*" Los Angeles, Calif.: Center for Futures Research, USC, 1974.

Helmer, O. *Social technology*. New York: Basic Books, 1966.

Henle, M. (Ed.). *Documents of gestalt psychology*. Berkeley, Calif.: University of California Press, 1961.

Huxley, A. *Brave new world*. New York: Harper & Row, 1969.

I Ching: the book of changes. Richard Wilhelm, translator and editor. Princeton, N.J.: Princeton University Press, 1950.

I Ching: the book of changes. John Blofeld, translator and editor. New York: Dutton, 1968.

Ittelson, W., and Cantril, H. *Perception, a transactional approach*. New York: Doubleday, 1954.

James, W. *Principles of psychology*. New York: Dover, 1950.

Jung, C. *Memories, dreams, and reflections*. New York: Pantheon, 1963.

Jung, C. *Modern man in search of a soul*. New York: Harcourt, Brace, Jovanovich, 1955.

Kahn, H., and Briggs, B. *Things to come*. New York: MacMillan, 1972.

Kahn, H., and Brown, W. "A world turning point." *The Futurist,* 1975, **9**(6):284–289.

Kahn, H., Brown, W., and Martel, L. *The next 200 years*. New York: Morrow, 1976.

Kahn, H., and Weiner, H. *The year 2000*. New York: MacMillan, 1967.

Kant, I. *The critique of Pure reason*. New York: Dutton, 1972.

Kaplan, A., Skogstad, A., and Gershick, M. "The prediction of social and technological events." *Public Opinion Quarterly,* 1950, **14**(1):93–110.

Katona, G. "Fifteen years of experience with measurement of consumer expectations." Proceedings of the Business and Statistics Section of the American Statistical Association, 1962.

Kelley, H. Attribution theory in social psychology. In D. Levine (Ed.). *Nebraska symposium on motivation, 1967*. Lincoln, Nebr.: University of Nebraska Press, 1967.

Koestler, A. *The roots of coincidence*. New York: Random House, 1972.

Kohler, W. *The mentality of apes*. New York: Liveright, 1976.

Krippner, S., Ullman, M., and Vaughn, A. *Dream telepathy*. New York: MacMillan, 1973.

Larsson, B. *Bayes strategies and human information seeking*. Lund, Universitet, Gleerup, Sweden, 1968.

Lewin, K. *A dynamic theory of personality*. New York: McGraw-Hill, 1935.

Lewin, K., Lippitt, R., and White, R. *Autocracy and democracy: an experimental inquiry*. New York: Harper & Row. 1960.

Lewin. K. *Field theory in social science*. New York: Harper & Row, 1951.

188   THE KNOWABLE FUTURE

Lewin, K. *Resolving social conflicts*. New York: Harper & Row, 1948.

London, I. "Some consequences for history and psychology of Langmuir's concept of convergence and divergence of phenomena." *Psychological Review*, 1946, **53**(3):170–188.

London, I. "Convergent and divergent amplification and its meaning for social science." *Psychological Reports*, 1977, 41, 111–123.

London, I., and Poltoratsky, E. "The problem of contemporary analysis in history and psychology." *Behavioral Science*, 1958, **3**(3):269–277.

Loye, D. *Adventues of a sunday psychic*. Work in progress.

Loye, D. *Journey into a pocket utopia*. Work in progress.

Loye, D. *The healing of a nation*. New York: Norton, 1971; Delta, 1972.

Loye, D. *The leadership passion: a psychology of ideology*. San Francisco, Calif.: Jossey-Bass, 1977.

Loye, D., Gorney, R., and Steele, G. Television effects: an experimental field study. *Journal of Communication*, 1977, 27:3, 206–216.

Loye, D., and Rokeach, M. "Ideology, belief systems, values, and attitudes." In Wolman, B. (Ed.). *International encyclopedia of neurology, psychiatry, psychoanalysis, and psychology*. New York: Van Nostrand Reinhold, 1976.

Luria, A. *The working brain*. New York: Basic Books, 1974.

Mankin, D. *Toward a post-industrial psychology*. New York: Wiley, in press.

Marx, K. *Economic and philosophic manuscripts of 1884*. New York: International, 1964.

Maslow, A. *Toward a psychology of being* (2nd Ed.). New York: Van Nostrand Reinhold, 1968.

McClelland, D. *The achieving society*. Princeton, N.J.: Van Nostrand, 1961.

McCully, R. "The Rorschach, synchronicity, and relativity." In R. Davis (Ed.). *Toward a discovery of the person*. Burbank, Calif.: The Society for Personality Assessment, 1974.

McGregor, D. *The human side of enterprise*. New York: McGraw-Hill, 1960.

McGregor, D. "The major determinants of the prediction of social events." *Journal of Abnormal and Social Psychology*, 1938, **33**:179–204.

McGuire, W. "The nature of attitudes and attitude change." In G. Lindsay and E. Aronson (Eds.). *The Handbook of Social Psychology* (Vol. 3). Reading, Mass.: Addison-Wesley, 1969.

Meadows, D. H., Meadows, D. L., Randers, J., and Behrens, W. *The limits to growth*. New York: Universe Books, 1972.

Messarovic, M., and Pestel, E. *Mankind at the turning point*. New York: Dutton, 1974.

Michael, D. Letter to the editor, *APA Monitor*, March 1977, p. 27.

Michael, D. (Ed.). *The future society*. New Brunswick, N.J.: Transaction Books, 1973.

Mihalasky, J., and Santa, M. "An improved Delphi method of group decision making: report on a research grant." On file, Parapsychology Foundation, New York, 1972.

Mill, J. *Principles of political economy*. Toronto: University of Toronto Press, 1965.

Miller, G., Gallanter, E., and Pribram, K. *Plans and the structure of behavior*. New York: Holt, Rinehart & Winston, 1960.

Mitchell, E. (Ed.) *Psychic exploration: a challenge for science*. New York: Putnam, 1974.

Moss, T. *The probability of the impossible*. Los Angeles, Calif.: Tarchor, 1974; Plume, 1975.

Mumford, L. *The condition of man*. Harcourt, Brace, Jovanovich, 1973.

Murphy, G. *The challenge of psychical research*. New York: Harper & Row, 1961.

Ornstein, R. *The psychology of consciousness*. San Francisco, Calif.: Freeman, 1972.

Orwell, G. *1984*. New York: New American Library, 1971.

Osgood, C. *An alternative to war or surrender*. Urbana, Ill.: University of Illinois Press, 1962.

Osgood, C., and Umpleby, S. "A computer-based system for exploration of possible futures for mankind 2000." In R. Jungk and J. Galtung (Eds.). *Mankind 2000. London: Allen & Unwin, 1969.*

Ostrander, S., and Schroeder, L. Psychic discoveries behind the iron curtain. New York: Prentice-Hall, 1970.

Packard, V. *The status seekers*. New York: McKay, 1959.

Parsons, T., Shils, E., Naegele, K., and Pitts, J. (Eds.). *Theories of society*. New York: Free Press, 1965.

Paul. "First epistle to the Corinthians," *The Dartmouth Bible*. Boston, Mass.: Houghton-Mifflin, 1950.

Pehek, J., Kyler, H., and Faust, D. "Image modulation in corona discharge photography," *Science*, 1976, **194**:263–270.

Piaget, J. *The psychology of intelligence*. New York: Harcourt, Brace, Jovanovich, 1950.

Plato. *The republic*. New York: Oxford University Press, 1945.

Pratt, J. *Parapsychology: an insider's view of ESP*. New York: Doubleday, 1964.

Progoff, I. *Jung, synchronicity, and human destiny*. New York: Julian Press, 1973.

Puthoff, H., and Targ, R. "Psychical phenomena and modern physics." In E. Mitchell (Ed.). *Psychic exploration*. New York: Putnam, 1974.

Riegel, K. "A manifesto for a dialectical psychology." *American Psychologist*, 1976, **31**(10):696–697.

Riegel, K. "Time and change in the development of the individual and society." In J. Gewirtz (Ed.). *Advances in child development and behavior* (Vol. 7). New York: Academic Press, 1972.

Roberts, M. "On the nature and condition of social science." *Daedalus*, 1974, **103**(3):47–64.

Rokeach, M. *The nature of human values*. New York: Free Press, 1973.

Sackman, H. *Delphi critique: expert opinion, forecasting, and group process*. Lexington, Mass.: Heath, 1975.

Schlesinger, A. "The tides of politics." In *Paths to the present*. Boston: Houghton-Mifflin, 1964.

Schmeidler, G. "Precognition scores related to the subject's ways of viewing time." *The Journal of Parapsychology*, 1964, **28.**

Schroeder, C. "The view from all over." *The Sciences*, 1974, **14**(10):6–11.

Sheldon, E., and Moore, W. *Indicators of social change: concepts and measurements*. New York: Russell Sage Foundation, 1968.

Sherif, M. "Experiments in group conflict." In S. Coopersmith (Ed.). *Frontiers of psychological research*. San Francisco, Calif.: Freeman, 1964.

Sherif, M. *The psychology of social norms*. New York: Harper & Row, 1936.

Sherif, M. "On the relevance of social psychology." *The American Psychologist*, 1970, **25**:144–156.

Skinner, B. *Verbal behavior*. New York: Appleton-Century-Crofts, 1957.

Smith, M. "Is psychology relevant to new priorities?" *American Psychologist*, 1973, **28**:463–471.

Sorokin, P. *Social and cultural dynamics*. New York: Bedminster Press, 1962.

Taff, B. "A memory of things to come." *Probe the Unknown,* 1977, **5**(2):53–60.

Taff, B. "Brain holograms: the light within." *Probe the Unknown,* 1973, **1**(6):26–31.

Taff, B. "Learned PSI: an exploration of parameters in a controlled study." Proceedings of Electro 76 Special Session "Psychotronics III, Institute of Electrical and Electronics Engineers," Boston, Mass., May 11–14, 1976.

Taquiri, R., and Petrullo, L. *Person perception and interpersonal behavior.* Stanford, Calif.: Stanford University Press, 1962.

Targ, R., and Puthoff, H. *Mind-reach.* New York: Delacorte Press, 1977

Theobald, R. *Futures conditional.* New York: Bobbs-Merrill, 1972.

Thibault, J., and Kelley, H. *Social psychology of groups.* New York: Wiley, 1959.

Toch, H. "The perception of future events: case studies in social prediction." *The Public Opinion Quarterly,* 1958, **22**(1):57–66.

Tomkins, S. "Affect and the psychology of knowledge." In S. Tomkins and C. Izard (Eds.). *Affect, cognition and personality.* New York: Springer, 1965.

Turoff, M. "Delphi conferencing: computer-based conferencing with anonymity." *Technological Forecasting and Social Change,* 1972, **3:**159–204.

Vaughan, A. *Patterns of prophecy.* New York: Hawthorn, 1973.

Vonnegut, K. *Player piano.* New York: Delacorte, 1971.

Watts, W. and Free, L. *State of the nation.* New York: Universe Books, 1973.

Weber, M. *Protestant ethic and the spirit of capitalism.* New York: Scribners, 1930.

Weber, M. "The social psychology of the world's religions." In T. Parsons, et al. (Eds.). *Theories of society.* New York: Free Press, 1965.

Westcott, M. *Toward a contemporary psychology of intuition.* New York: Rinehart & Winston, 1968.

Wooldridge, D. *The machinery of the brain.* New York: McGraw-Hill, 1963.

Young, M. *The rise of the meritocracy, 1870–2033: an essay on education and equality.* London: Thomas and Hudson, 1958.

INDEX

Abolitionist, 86
The Achieving Society, 9, 44
Active society, 152
Activism-inactivism, 44, 72, 75, 77, 78, 83, 105, 160, 163
Adams, Brooks, 5, 69, 132, 133, 137, 138
Adams, Henry, 5, 6, 16, 17, 22, 69, 124, 131, 132, 146
Adams, John Quincy, 4, 69, 88, 132, 133, 138, 141, 150, 151
Advanced potential theory, 63, 140
Agnew, Spiro, 124, 125
Alienation, 72, 153, 158
Alternative futures, 7, 24
American Dream, 150, 154
Ames, Adelbert, 78
Anomie, 72, 153, 158
Antithesis, 33
Apperception, 132
Arabs, 157
Archetypes, 63
Art of Conjecture, The, 13, 14, 15, 89
Asch, Solomon, 15
Assertive Tendency, 63
Assimilation and accommodation, 40
Astrologers, 59
Attention, 35
Attitudes, 27, 31, 42, 43, 73, 91, 126
Attitude and values change, 31
Attribution theory, 36
Augustinian Age, 18, 30, 34, 134
Authoritarianism, 157
"Awesome transformation," 135
Azimov, Isaac, 21

Balanced or stable state society, 17, 23
Baysian inference, 36
Bell, Daniel, 7, 16, 134
Bender, Hans, 59

Benezet, Anthony, 83
Berger, Hans, 37
Bessent, Malcolm, 55
Bible, 51
Big government issue, *see* Governmental power issue
Birney, James, 69, 87, 88
Bioplasma, 62
Blake, William, 22
Boulding, Kenneth, 23
Brain function, 51
Branching points, 16
Brave New World, 154
Brier, Robert, 54, 64, 138
Bronfenbrenner, Urie, 30
Brookings Institute, 151
Brown, Harrison, 23
Brown, Jerry, 97, 102, 108, 109, 112, 113, 114, 115, 120
Brown, John, 85, 87
Bruner, Jerome, 39, 40
Business, and Carter's campaign appeals to, 116
  cotton's big business impact on history, 133, 134
  cycles (boom and bust, bull and bear), 128
  Delphi forecasting techniques, use of, 46, 47
  Dynamic-Hasty type, as successful decision-maker, 57, 58
  environment issue, sensitivity to, 95, 100
  and executive ESP studies, 56, 57, 58, 60
  executive strike of 1980, 151
  forecasting, criteria for doing own versus employing consultants, 161
  favorable future use of, 151

191